A SPORTSMAN'S
LIFE

H. WOODROW WARD

TATE PUBLISHING
AND ENTERPRISES, LLC

Published by Tate Publishing & Enterprises, LLC
127 E. Trade Center Terrace | Mustang, Oklahoma 73064 USA
1.888.361.9473 | www.tatepublishing.com

Tate Publishing is committed to excellence in the publishing industry. The company reflects the philosophy established by the founders, based on Psalm 68:11,
"The Lord gave the word and great was the company of those who published it."

Book design copyright © 2014 by Tate Publishing, LLC. All rights reserved.
Cover design by Rodrigo Adolfo
Interior design by Jake Muelle

Published in the United States of America

ISBN: 978-1-62854-164-9
1. Sports & Recreation / General
2. Biography & Autobiography / Personal Memoirs
13.11.13

DEDICATION

———➤●◄———

Dedicated to all of the local Rod and Gun Clubs scattered throughout the United States, started by men like the Major and kept alive in the spirit of hard work and a love for *A Sportsmen's Life* that only those of like affliction can understand.

DEDICATION

"BELONGING"

Turning from his friends
Where the conversation continues uninterrupted,
He walks slowly towards the line

Drinking in the sweet aromas of oil and leather

Number 2? He queries the trapper.
No, he is answered mechanically, number 4.
The shotgun still perched on his shoulder
He nods to his rivals
Standing confidently among men

Thoroughly enjoying this interlude in life.

The weight is right and balances precisely in his hands.
The rhythm is different and yet always the same,
Call! Squeeze! Rest. Call! Squeeze! Rest.
A familiar crack in his ears, the abrupt bounce against his shoulder.
The action is opened and a smoking case removed

Releasing spent propellant rafting upward to be savored.

Each shooter stands restless,
Waiting expectantly for their turn
Keeping silent count of their score.

Nervously fingering the heavy cases bulging the pockets.

The sounds echo, the commands unnecessary;
End! Walk! The Trapper reads the scores, 4, 5, 5, 4, 3.
The choreograph complete, the squad has moved
"Ready on one!" the shooter calls.
The rhythm begins anew

There is a great peace to be found in belonging
To a place and to a time
Where like-minded men
Share their passion for a tradition
Passed down the years
By many others who walked the line before them.

THE END: AN INTRODUCTION

N ot so many years ago, I met a man unlike any I
   had met before, a man born of my grandfather's
generation. A man who treated me graciously and who,
over the far-to-brief-of time we had together, I grew
to admire deeply. He lived by a code of honor, loyalty,
and hard work and a man who felt led, for whatever
reason, to share his passion for the sportsman's life
with a lonely stranger, forever changing my life and my
life's perspective.

Having mustered out of the Army Corps of
Engineers the previous September, I'd taken the
position of project manager for a developer who'd
bought out what was described to me as a defunct old
gun club. With no family ties and no other offers to
speak of coming my way, I loaded my assembled earthly
belongings—which means I threw my duffle, two large
tool boxes and collection of work boots—into the back
of a pick-up and drove the few hundred odd miles
down here at the end of winter.

Here by the way is Delphia—a little town midway
between a couple not-so-little towns that were still too
small to be called cities, but large enough to support
some serious employment. That made Delphia one of
those places people wanted to raise their families, in
other words a typical twenty-first-century suburb—
social life centers on dance lessons, soccer and little

league. The big-box hardware stores were here as were the ubiquitous eateries serving food off of plastic menus with different names that managed somehow to all taste exactly the same. All of this new enough however, to hint at what the area was like when there were more tractors licensed in the county than Beamers.

So here I was, Robert Lloyd Grant, dusty and dirty, new to the area and to civilian life. The fresh-out-of-service feeling like I was just on leave, having recently been cured by the absence of a regular paycheck from good Ol' Uncle Sam, hitting me hard. I've kinda grown accustomed to eating on a regular basis so I found a job coordinating contractors who would turn this unused property into something that would pass for a housing development complete with cul-de-sacs, sidewalks, and cutesy road signs like Bluebird Circle and Honeybee Avenue.

I had only been in the new job a few months, still stumbling my way around a strange town and trying hard to acclimate to civilian living. So I was completely unprepared that day in late summer when I cut the last of the crew loose, for just how abruptly all of that was about to change.

The car came slowly down the long drive. Even with the window barely cracked he could still smell the sweet perfume of spruce, honeysuckle and lilac. The dogwoods were past their annual explosion of color and summer was well under way.

A sudden breeze came up from the direction of the spring-fed pond, and he caught the familiar fragrance of still algae-crested water. Was it really still there, he thought? He avoided looking directly down the lane in its direction but a weary smile crept across his face anyway as faded images of so many cool, damp April days fishing for stocked trout with the kids came into his mind's eye. The kids were always an important part of the club. Laughing and slipping in the mud as they stared intently at those red and white bobbers floating in the wind until their eyes watered!

He shook himself free of the shadows, straightened up in the seat, tightened his grip on the steering wheel, and drove quickly past to ensure the memories would not linger. A red squirrel barked loudly from the branches of a felled oak while the resident blue jay bounced from brush pile to brush pile as if leading him to his destination. At the end of the drive, he turned the vehicle slowly into the vacant lot, the gravel crunching softly under the tires as he turned sharply to park, working the wheel hard to avoid the deepest of ruts.

The parking lot, once crowded with pick-ups, SUVs and men from all walks of life had degenerated into a staging area for heavy equipment, rank with the smell of diesel fuel and lubricants. Its ground stained from the leaking behemoths whose black oils mixed with recent rain to present a bleak and mournful landscape before him.

It was an old model sedan, faded blue but clean, except for the thick dust thrown up by the departing heavy equipment operators, fast for the first beer of the night. The driver parked his car in the shade of an ancient maple branded with a large red X spray painted by the commercial forester so the loggers would be sure to take it down and salvage the wood. These guys won't let any tree larger than twelve inches in girth standing. Not one.

He sat quietly in his car facing away from the old trap field as if he really didn't want to get out. The door opened deliberately though not very enthusiastically, and for a moment I thought there was someone sitting beside him. I squinted into the sunlight to try and see if there was a passenger, but before I could focus beyond the old man, the door closed. If there was someone with him, they were hidden from my prying eyes by the setting sun.

With the hot summer sun hanging low in a cloudless sky and still stinging my eyes, I stopped for a second as it suddenly occurred to me, after all the days I had been working here, this field faces east. I had heard it was a trap field, you know where they launch some sort of disc targets out for some guy to shoot at with a shotgun. Was the field really set up so shooters didn't have to contend with the setting evening sun? Naw, couldn't be. Who'd go to all that trouble just to shoot some targets?

Slowly the old man lifted his head to look at the old trap field. With a deep, staggered breath as if he was visiting a dying friend, he took it all in. The trap houses that protected the large hopper-fed machines designed to throw clay targets seventy yards downfield gone, the electricity cut. Those carefully painted houses constructed of concrete block laid by a member-mason, now waiting in piles for the front loader and dump truck to carry them off to a landfill.

The field itself with it's carefully tended grass dutifully maintained by retirees who kept it free from crabgrass and dandelions: tore apart, rutted, and muddy from the big machines. He took it all in. The robins were finding it easy to fill themselves with worms from the freshly overturned earth.

"Good"! he said out loud to no one in particular. "At least something is finding a way to make use of this mess!"

Several times he started toward the field, then stopped as if he had forgotten or maybe remembered something. He walked slowly but directly to the pile of broken block that was the second of four houses, a white number two could be seen on one of the pieces stacked on the pile. He stood weakly before the heap, his shoulders slumped and head drooped betraying the pain he suffered in seeing this place all tore up.

He carried what appeared to be a hat in one of his hands. I expected him to put it on and protect that old grey head from the sun and the swarms of gnats flying around him adding to his torment. *Just some old man*, I thought with nothing better to do on a hot summer afternoon. Heck, I bet he's as old as that big ol' maple he just parked under.

I waited behind my pick-up pretending to mess with some tools just to see if he'd put that funny old hat on, but he didn't. He carried it loosely in his hand turning it over and over without ever once looking at it. After a few moments he reached down to brace himself against the pile of rubble that once stood plum and strong against the weather and then slowly lowered himself down on to the block.

I watched the old man from the shadows of the tree line as he painfully lowered himself onto the heap of broken block to rest, my high-riding, one-ton pick-up shielding me from his gaze, or so I thought. I was transfixed for the time, feeling a little bit like a trespasser or voyeur. *Who is he* or better still, *who was he?* Why did he come here to this old field, this defunct gun club? I can't explain why I cared or why I would even want to know.

According to the developer that hired me, the old club had been deteriorating for years. First, the trap fields and rifle ranges were closed and after that the remaining members who were made up mostly of archers and fisherman found they just couldn't raise enough money to pay the taxes and keep the property up to code. When he hired me he said, with a look of a soulless-banker about to close on a foreclosure: "I guess they must've had one to many free clinics or just couldn't charge enough at their events to meet the rising costs of utilities, insurance and stuff. Crap happens, huh?"

Down at the roadhouse I frequented from time to time, I heard my "enterprising" boss got the property with a little help from a friend on the board of commissioners and all for back taxes. All he had to do then was hire a guy like me to keep the contractors in line and lay out a sub-division at $100,000 per 100 ft by 150 ft lot. Not a bad business plan really. High profit, low risk, and no real capital since the property was offered as the collateral for his real estate loan; he wasn't even using his own cash! Pretty cool deal, really. I approached the old man slowly. I could now see the hat he carried was tattered and ripped. It looked as though someone had shot a large hole right through the middle of it. How odd is that? I moved slowly down to where he was seated, not wanting to startle him, but I was the one that jumped when without even turning around he said more or less to me, "Spent many hours here a good part of my life, good times mostly, aggravating times too." He shook his head and drew a haggard breath before continuing with a strained effort, "Friends, competitors, teammates, a lot of faces burned into an old man's mind. Hard memories to let die, hard memories," his voice trailing off, "you didn't leave with the others, why not?"

I wasn't prepared for such a direct question. All I could do was stutter back at him in self-defense. "I, uh…I was just wondering, you know, what you were doing out here or why anyone would come out to this property now?"

"Humph!" He grunted, "*this property!* This little piece of old farm ground is just a place on a sectional map to you and your boss, but to me, to my friends, to those of us who built it, this was *our* place! A safe place! A refuge from the daily routine, a plot of land near home where men of like-minded passion met to shoot, to compete and to pass along that same passion to whoever wanted to share it."

Passion? I echoed more to myself than to the old man. "Sir," I said, "I don't think I understand?"

"No," he said flatly and without turning my way. "No sir, I guess you don't at that. How could you?"

Without looking up at me or saying anything more, he struggled to his feet and walked out to some loose dirt in the middle of the field. With great effort, he bent down to rest on his knees and then carefully buried that old hat.

Satisfied that the hat was properly at rest, he stood up, dusted off his pants, straightened himself properly to leave with dignity, and solemnly turned his back on the ravaged field with a finality of ceremony; then and only then did he walk directly to his car.

He passed within a few feet of me without acknowledgment, lost in the pain of his memories. The strain of emotion was showing in every line of that old face when suddenly and to this day I have no idea why, I felt an overwhelming desire to know what this was all about. I knew I couldn't let him leave without asking, asking what I wasn't even sure of right then, but I had to know more about this man and this old gun club. Why did he come out here, now? And what, for crying out loud was all that about burying that old hat in a tore up trap field anyway? Why would anyone really care what was going on out here after all these years?

I easily caught the elderly old man as he limped slowly back to his car and latched onto his arm. "What is this place to you old man?" I demanded.

Leaning heavily on the roof of the car, he shook his head and looked away past the trap field, past the demolished trap houses and past the rutted parking lot. With the fragrance of the cooling pond rafting upwards to where we stood, he was looking back to another time. Closing his moistening eyes, he whispered in a low thoughtful voice, "I doubt you'd understand young man."

"No sir," I replied honestly, "I might not, but there has to be a reason you came out here today, in this hot sun. I mean more than just to bury some moth-eaten old hat. I've got some time, and I'd like to hear about it. I'm pretty new in Delphia and don't know anything about it outside of sub-dividing and building. It looks like this old place must've really meant something to you, huh? I mean, I'd like to know a little more about it and why or how it could mean so much to someone like you, if you could stick around a bit?"

He hesitated and I could see his mind working as he sized me up. He stole a glance into the car at his passenger and finally, reluctantly he said softly, "Okay, as he let himself scan the old field one more time. If you're truly interested, I'll share the story of the old Delphia Fish, Game and Gun Club. It's really more about the men who built it though not the real estate. It's all about guys that cared for, fought over and genuinely loved it for over sixty years."

I looked back at what once was the Trap field, scanning the coarse field, the felled trees and rutted logging paths, I tried to see what the old man saw, but I couldn't, I didn't have his vision. No, it was painfully clear that what he was seeing were shadows really filtered in a sepia-colored montage created by many years of hard work, deep passion, and haunting memories of friends now gone.

A PLACE TO SHOOT

—————⟫●⟪—————

The old man and I just stood there for a few minutes by his car. He had to let the emotion of his afternoon subside, the pain still visible on his face. He was also sizing me up, absorbing our conversation. I'm sure he was questioning my sincerity, after all a dirty young man comes out of the shadows and invades a very private moment. Not the norm in way of introduction regardless the circumstance!

It was hot for that time of day, and the sweat began to stream down his face. He reached into his pocket for a handkerchief to towel-off and said in a formal kinda voice: "So you want to know about this place, do you?"

"Yes sir, I do. Really," I replied. "The name's Bob Grant, I'm the foreman here."

"Well, Bob Grant foreman here, if you want to know, *really*," he replied drawling out the words and for the first time since he arrived permitting himself a slight smile. "Guess I'll have to go back to the very beginning. Let's go over here on the bank. I'll grab a couple of cans of soda I have here in the trunk, and there's still plenty of shade under this ol' maple. Won't be the first time I told a few tales while sitting on this piece of dirt!"

I eagerly accepted the cold drink all the while secretly wishing it was brewed malt instead of brewed tea. But since it didn't look like I'd be getting anything stronger for a while and being as it had been a long hot day and I was a thirsty, dirty young man who just wanted to sit down, I accepted his generosity and found a place on the grass near my new friend.

We opened our drinks, and I watched the old man as he turned the thoughts around in his head as his eyes glassed over a bit and then his face turned from the sour disgust of a man saying good-bye to the bright attentive look of someone with something to say.

"It was right after the war, early in 1946," he began slowly. "The servicemen were returning to the states and most just wanted to get busy doing all the things they could only dream about while stationed overseas. College for some thanks to the new G.I. Bill, work for others and making babies for most!" He blushed red as I stared in amazement at his innocence!

Turning serious again, he said, "Pre-war America was a tough place to live. We were still recovering from the Great Depression and most Americans had little time for themselves. Each day was work and struggle, scrimp, and save. Things like hunting and fishing were just looked upon as an extension of all of the other effort that went into putting food on the table. Everyone had a garden, many families had chickens and some even had a hog or other livestock. Depended mainly on how much space you had, not so much as where you lived. Shucks...*I never met anyone that actually said shucks before! People nowadays would have a fit or call their lawyer if they had seen what the good citizens of Delphia kept at there homes!* Like I said young man, a very tough time."

"Well," he continued as if he was comfortable giving a lecture, "the war changed all of that. Men came back and found that their families had been working hard long hours at defense jobs and many even had savings accounts. Imagine that—bills were all paid with something left over for a rainy day! We had no idea how good we were going to have it! How could we have known?" His voice trailed off and he slowly shook his head while looking down and kicking at the dirt, he repeated himself in a whisper, "how could we have known?" And then looked me straight in the eye, "No way we could have known, no way."

"Well sir," he said as he found himself, "the men who grew up chasing game with their Model 12 Winchester's, LC Smith's, and Savage pumps still had the desire and now they had the time to shoot during the off season too! These men came home to families and waiting jobs, still carrying months of back pay and Uncle Sam's generous '52-20' dollars for anyone that wanted it. They survived a long, miserable war and were ready to enjoy the lives they could only dream about not long before.

"These were the men who pulled together to form small clubs like this one all over the country. Around here, there seemed to be a little club with a trap field, a pond, and a rifle range for every post office! These weren't the elite clubs of the aristocrats in New York or California where the rich and famous shot custom guns, wore fitted shooting clothes, had a paid staff to man the traps, cut the grass, and polish the members' boots! No sir! At these little clubs you'd find railroaders,

masons, carpenters, barbers, and shop keepers. We didn't use terms like *white collar* or *blue collar* either; you were what you did, simple as that! When you step up to the sixteen-yard line at trap or take aim at the annual turkey shoot, no one checked your union card!

"Here in Delphia the idea for a club was brought up by the Major," he continued uncomfortably as he fidgeted a bit on the hard dirt. "Can't recall just what he was called...before the war, but after he got back it was the Major from then on.

"Before enlisting in the army, he was a teacher at the local high school. And... What? No I don't remember what he taught," the old man barked. Try to keep up, will ya son?

"Anyway, it was the Major's wife who wrote to him about the farm when he was stationed in England two years earlier in the spring of 44. She visited the farmer who owned this property with some other ladies from the church when the farmer fell ill and then learned he had no children or close relatives and..."

"How did they know he was sick?" I interrupted, now totally into the story.

"They're women son, they just know! We're never going to get done here if you keep asking those kind of questions. It's getting late, and I should be getting along."

"Okay, okay, I'll keep quiet," I apologized. "You were saying the Major was in England in the spring of 1944."

"Yes, spring 1944." He paused for a few seconds, and I thought I lost him for sure, but he sorta snorted to

himself, obviously remembering something he'd rather have forgotten and then got on with the story.

"Yes, um spring 1944," he repeated with emphasis and sitting up a bit straighter. "His wife mentioned the farm in one of her letters. The rolling hills, the spring-fed pond, and all those trees! 'Why didn't he sell them to the mill and pay off the bank?' she wrote, telling him how she questioned the farmer that day.

'No,' the farmer said flatly, 'these trees been here long as I have, and they are going to be here long after I'm gone if I have anything to say about it!'

"All through the last months of the war the Major thought about that farm. He remembered hunting rabbits on it with some of the guys he knew from his school days but wouldn't it be nice to have a place set aside for shooting and maybe a little hunting? Run the beagles every now and then during the late summer to get them in shape for November.

"Well, if nothing else, the army taught him that things didn't just come to you. If you wanted it, you go get it, whether it was a two story chalet needed for artillery observation or a farm back home for shooting clay targets in the summer and the deer rifles each December. He knew he'd need help, and he already made a mental list of conspirators before ever reaching home. All during the trip across the Atlantic, he thought about that farm."

The old man paused here, closed his eyes and for a minute I swore he was swaying back and forth as if he was in a ship. And again just when I thought I'd lost him he shook himself back to the present.

"That's right," he pressed on now showing signs of fatigue from all the memories, "all the way home he thought about that farm and as soon as he got back, well okay, after some overdue time with the missus he looked up his old friends as well as some of the local hunters he'd met at the hardware store where they bought their license and shells and pitched his idea."

The old man recited a virtual roll call of charter members, "There was Skip Davis. Ol' Skip and I used to chase cottontails and the occasional grouse before Skip was drafted. We called on Heath Roberts, the high school principal and the Major's boss before the war to help keep us young'uns in line, you know," he said, lowering his voice as if it were a piece of gossip. "He was the only man we knew at that time that had an honest-to-goodness shooting jacket! Well, he'd brought it out a time or two at the volunteer fireman's turkey shoot and seemed to be worn at all the right places. We knew he'd want in on a place to shoot. Besides, what we heard of his college days, we suspected Mr. Roberts might know a thing or two about running the place."

There were others, my new friend recalled, "Curt Lauver, Joe Williams and his brother Bill, Petie Nelson, and Shorty McGray. All good men, good hunters, and more than one of 'em a good dog-man to boot!"

Leaning forward a bit and in a whisper, the old man said, "Most of them good ol' boys fished a bit too, but that was mainly to get out of the chores all the women kept thinking up for us to do!"

We both laughed at the thought of these hardened men ducking their wives like school boys, just to sit along the pond or some small creek with a couple of cold bottles and a wicker creel by their sides.

First, the Major had to go to the farm and reach an agreement with the owner. The farmer had to sell, no question, so he pitched his plan to him and when he learned the details of the Major's plan, the old farmer was all for it. To meet his debt, he needed to walk away with $1,800. *A gift*, the Major thought! It was in reach!

Now the old man had an excitement in his voice that even had my heart pounding, so much that I didn't even realize that I was crushing the ice tea can!

Of course, there were meetings at the Delphia Tavern and of course they argued over dues, rules, a name for the club and who'd be the first president. And of course, they all knew it would be the Major, after all it was his idea. "Just seemed right" was all my new friend would offer when I asked how he was elected.

"Well, Bob Grant foreman here," the old man said, now visibly worn out from the rigors of the lengthy tale. "It's getting late and I have to get the missus home. If you want to hear more about this place you can find me at the Village Apartments where the old Stoner Farm used to sit. Kinda enjoyed talken' to ya this afternoon. Wouldn't mind picking it up again sometime."

I thanked him for his time, helped him to his feet, and made sure he didn't stumble getting to his car. Without much thought I said offhandedly, "Sounds great sir. I'll take you up on that. How about Sunday?"

"Sure," he said thoughtfully, "Sunday after church around one o'clock will be good for me. My wife takes a bit of a nap then, and we can sit out back by the fountain."

He got into his car, turned the engine over, and started to back out. "Wait!" I yelled.

Rolling the window down with effort and in a careful whisper so as not to disturb his passenger, he asked, "What now son? I'm tired."

"I don't know your name. How will I find your apartment?"

He looked over at his elderly passenger, who I could now see was a woman fast asleep, looking to be about the same age as the old man. He slowly turned back towards me and with a sly smile I'd seen so many times over the past hour simply said, "Just ask for the Major," and off he drove.

WELCOME

———⟫●⟪———

I was glad the old man didn't want to meet until Sunday afternoon. Not that I was attending any church like he and his wife were. No, I knew I'd be feeling a bit wasted from my end-of-week ritual down at the Roadhouse and wouldn't even see noon.

I work hard all week and want to relax and forget about the grind of responsibility on the weekend. That's what Saturdays are for, right? Work hard, play hard—we always said in the Army. I wondered if that had anything to do with these old guys and their *club* as the Major called it. I'm sure all the men worked hard during the week, so I really don't see why they'd want to have a place like that where, after they did their regular work and the upkeep of their own homes, they'd come out to that place and work some more—*weird!*

I pulled into the Village Retirement complex expecting to find it depressing and smelling of mothballs, but it wasn't like I'd imagined an old-folks home would be at all. There were elderly adults there for sure, canes, walkers and hearing aids, but they were still able to get around okay and seemed to enjoy each others company.

Walking up to the door, I asked the couple sitting just outside the entrance where I might find the Major. They asked if I was a relative and when I said, "No, just a friend," I caught a suspicious glance that passed

between them before they hesitantly pointed me around
to the back of the building. I couldn't really blame them
for being cautious. After all dressed the way I was, in
old jeans and my tee shirt hanging out over my belt, I
didn't exactly fit in with these neatly dressed retirees.
There are still a lot of lowlife in the world that would
try to take advantage of the weak and elderly, though
I can't imagine the Major being taken by anyone. He
seemed pretty sharp to me.

I worked my way around to the back of the white
brick, single-floor building, past the rose bushes and
bird feeders placed where homebound residents could
see them from their apartments until I found the Major
resting in a neat little garden with a fountain right in
the middle of it. He was sitting on a lawn chair, pillow
stuffed low behind his back and a pitcher of lemonade
with two glasses filled with ice within reach. I stared
intently at the old man as I approached slowly from
his left. Even sitting quietly he appeared purposeful
and focused; a long-sleeve sweater over a polo shirt—
though the day was warm and the air calm—dark green
khaki pants and not-so-worn walking shoes.

So this guy was one of the founders of the club,
and to hear him tell it, one of the chief instigators? I
wonder what kind of man he is or was, or whatever
the case maybe. Well, I would see what I found out
today, it should prove to be entertaining if nothing else.
Nothing better to do.

As I approached, the Major turned and stood up
slowly to greet me, trying to hide the pain and stiff back
with a quick smile. Moving around obviously required

some effort for the old man, but he seemed genuinely glad I was there. He extended his hand with a broad smile, which I took gingerly not wanting to hurt him.

"Wasn't sure you were going to make it," he said lightly, "I know what it's like to work hard all week and well, I thought you might lose interest after I'd left the club the other day."

"Nah," I said, "working out there the rest of the week just made me more curious about the place and what went on out there."

I moved around and stood in front of the other chair and before the Major could even sit back down I started in bluntly, "So you were the founder, huh?" He smiled again, motioned for me to sit and after I was situated he carefully filled my glass. Judging from the condition of the ice he hadn't been waiting long. I caught him out of the corner of my eye waiting to see my reaction as I sipped his wife's homemade lemonade.

"Very good," I said while secretly hoping that it wouldn't have an issue with the Jack and Coke still settling from the night before.

"Well," he began as he started to settle back down onto the chair, "I guess your crew is making good progress for the developer? He'll want to get all the foundations poured and the houses already sold under roof before frost gets hold of the ground so your finishing guys can work indoors over the winter."

I was taken aback at his frank, direct comments, especially after all the emotion he showed at the Club earlier in the week. "Yeah," I replied simply, "we're making steady headway, pretty much right on schedule thanks to the dry summer."

"I won't lie," he said, "I'll miss the club, but you know, it was a heck of a lot of work." Then turning uncomfortably in his chair, he stopped abruptly to reposition the pillow. After it appeared to be satisfactorily nestled back into place I picked up the conversation.

"Yeah, I was thinking about that on the way over here. I know you guys had to have worked hard all week at your regular jobs and then you'd have to make time to take care of your own homes. Why in the world would you want to have a place like the Club that you had to keep up, on top of everything else?"

This volley of thought came out quickly and all in a single breath which obviously surprised the elderly Major. He just kinda stared at me without blinking. I felt a bead of sweat forming and then I was the one turning uncomfortably in my chair.

"So, I continued as I watched the Major size me up. You came home from the war, you called all your buddies to sell them on this idea and then you got the property and the Club started."

"Whoa, Bob, I hope I haven't given you the wrong impression, he said seriously, there seems to be an awful lot of *you*, meaning *me* in what you just spouted out there. I laid the ground work and even brought the original members together, but transforming that old farm into a decent Club took a lot of hard work from a lot of good people."

"Well," I said, "that might be a good place to start. Tell me about some of them."

He leaned his head back gently to gather his thoughts when suddenly he stiffened and caught the movement of a bird-food stealing squirrel scurrying up a pole, then remembering he wasn't alone looked back at me a little sheepishly, "Once a hunter always a hunter, huh?"

"Uh, yeah, I guess so," I replied having no idea what he meant.

He kicked around some dirt at his feet and cleared his throat a few times, took another long slow sip of the lemonade and began slowly, "I guess the best way to tell you about the Club is just to relate some of the things that have stayed with me over the years, some of the high points, tough times, fun times, friends made, and his voice quivering, "some lost." He grew silent for a moment and," he grimaced noticeably.

"You see the thing about running a club, a business, or a company of infantry for that matter is that it takes a lot of boring mundane, day in and day out work. No secret, no magic formula; just precious time, sweat and hard work, pure and simple! But like in everyone's life, there are those red letter days too when it all seems so clear and so worth while."

"Oka," I said, "tell me about one of those red letter days, Major."

He laughed, "Sorry son, I can get kind of preachy. The wife really lets me have it sometimes!" We laughed again.

He hesitated while he re-grouped his thoughts, "Okay let's try this he said turning in his seat towards me, it's a bit corny but I think it might work since you've been on the property for a time and at least know the lay of the land."

"Try what?" I asked reluctantly.

"I'm gonna give you the welcome tour I used to give all new members to the club when we first got started, you game?"

"Yeah, well all right," I slurred, taken aback a bit and looking around to see if this was a joke playing out at my expense with someone watching behind a window curtain.

"Great, let's get going!" he said with enthusiasm as his voice took on a new energy.

"Hello, you can call me Major. I'm glad you decided to join our little club here along the mountain. Glad to see you're wearing your walkin' shoes too. I want to get you a'quainted with the grounds so you won't run into no trouble with the neighbors."

"Hmmm," I muttered under my breath, still a bit suspicious of this little skit of his and the sudden regression of his grammar.

"Right, okay then", he said clearing his throat again deliberately and ignoring my stare. "Let's start over here by the pond. It's filling in nicely now that we've had some rain. We stocked it with about a'hundurd trout and t'urty or so bass and a few carp and catty's for good measure. It's mainly for the kids, but you're welcome to use it if you want, just throw the bass back. We want them to get big and fat!

"The trout won't make it to Fall anyway, just not enough flow to keep the temperature down below sixty-five and oxygen levels up for'em all summer. So don't feel guilty 'bout takin a few for dinner some night."

"Was that true?" I interrupted. "The fish are really that hard to keep?"

"Of course it's true", he frowned as he lowered his voice. "Do you think I make this stuff up?"

Anyway, he continued in his authoritative voice, "be careful with the snappers, we've got some big-ins' in there. Saw one of 'em take a duckling last spring!"

"Aw come on," I said, "a duckling? Really?"

"You questioning my integrity young man?"

"Uh, no, sorry. I just…"

"Just leave the tour to me please?"

"Over yonder there are the archery bales. Got some guys who like to extend their season and get out early to see where the big boys are hanging."

"The what?" I asked desperately lost.

"The deer with the best antlers," he said, shaking his head.

"We got a good patch of raspberries back there and you're welcome to them same as anyone else but if you go back to pick'em make sure you leave a hat or shirt on the bale. That way the guys will yell at-cha before they cut loose and give you time to get out' the way.

"Now let's walk back up the road here a piece where you came in at the gate. You see here where the driveway turns into the woods. We'll we need to walk out 'bout two-hundurd yards to where the rifle ranges are set up. Here we are, right now we have a hundurd and a fifty yard range. Use the benches and sandbags and don't do anything stupid like shootin' mid- range.

We don't want any ricochets flying over the backstop. The farmers 'round here get a might ticked when lead falls into their livestock.

"We can cut through the trees over there. I want to take you back to the edge of the property. Here, you see this old fence line running along the ridge? Yeah? Well don't cross it. Mr. Kauffman ain't real tickled that we got this property and is looking for any excuse he can dream up to cause us grief with the county.

"We have about three-hundurd acres all told and you're welcome to run your dogs in the summer but wait till the hens are off their nests, and the fawns are running with the does. Some of us hunt small game after work while the light lasts through early October and a few of the guys will come back late in the deer season to see if anything worthwhile has been pushed up from the farms. But if you hunt out here, remember to watch where ya are and where your bullet and shot is going to stop if you shoot. We don't want any accidents, okay?

"Let's head back to the trap field. We have two traps now, but plan to expand if there's any interest. We shoot Monday's from May to September and then close it down for huntin' season. What do you mean you're not a trap shooter? If you got a workable twelve gauge, you're a trap shooter! We shoot until dusk and then go out and pick up the unbroken birds so we can use them again. Saves us some money on birds, and depending on who is doing the shooting, sometimes it's a lot of money!" He leaned back and laughed out loud! I laughed too but had no idea why!

He took a few minutes to collect himself, closed his eyes, and smiled obviously reflecting on the old club he remembered: the tree lined driveway, his friends gathered around tailgates and trucks in various states of repair, talking guns, dogs, and politics. Then after another sip of his wife's lemonade, he looked over at me, rattled the ice in his glass; I could almost sense him willing me to understand his deep feelings about this place "Well son, what do you think of our little club?"

I took a deep breath and looked around nervously trying to avoid the Major's twinkling blue eyes. There was just so much going through my mind, images of this past week as I watched my crew finish draining and back-filling the pond, bulldozing the trap fields that will become some guy's backyard and drag what was left of the archery bales and rifle targets onto a pile where they burned slowly before the front-loader scooped it all up in one gulp.

Fighting to contain my own emotions from deep within that I didn't understand and trying not to show any of it to the Major, I swallowed hard and whispered through clenched teeth, "Just fine, Major. Thanks for the tour. When can I meet the other members?"

"Next time, Bob Grant," the Major said softly closing his eyes. "Next time."

MR. TRAP

———➤●◄———

I visited the Major several more times during the end
of summer, always meeting on Sunday afternoon
out back by the garden at the retirement home, where
he told me about the work he and his friends did to
transform the old farm into a sportsmans' club: clearing
trees and hauling clean dirt for the backstop at the rifle
ranges, how they dredged the pond with rowboats
pulling heavy chains to keep the water flowing, and then
the work they did to convert the old log home into a
clubhouse where they held monthly meetings and kept
the few files they had with members' names, addresses
etc. The day-to-day mundane things he always talked
about during our first visits.

Several weeks passed after Labor Day before I could
return to the Major's and with Fall fast approaching I
had to be sure we had all of the prep work that required
heavy equipment completed at the club site—that isn't
what the developer calls it, but it's what it will be to me
from now on, the club site—with all of the building
lots surveyed and perked. During my last visit, I asked
if he would tell me more about some of the members,
particularly the men who helped him develop and
maintain the club.

By the time, I finally made it back to see the Major
it was a gloomy rainy day so sitting out by the fountain
was out. I think the fountain meetings, which we took

to calling them, was something he looked forward to as much as I did, judging by the way he was always waiting for me, pillow behind his back and lemonade by his side. This week would be different though, I would have to venture into his apartment.

I entered uncontested after sprinting from the parking lot through the cold rain finally slowing to a fast walk as I reached the door and into the quiet lobby. The residents, now used to seeing me on a more-or-less regular basis, dressed in my typical weekend clothes of old jeans, sneakers, and tee shirt, greeted me warmly. These gentle, sometimes forgotten adults who sit in the lobby to escape their tiny apartments for a few hours, nodded, and smiled as I walked briskly by them. I tried to return their smile as I passed but the future, perhaps my future, is tough to acknowledge on a dark rainy day.

I found the Major's apartment and knocked softly, remembering that his wife reportedly took a nap at this time, so I was mildly surprised when the door opened and it was she, not the Major greeting me. "Hello," she said in a soft but warm voice. "How are you today?" A small-framed, grey-haired, grandmotherly type wearing a pink cotton dress and white apron with a large, red apple embroidered on it. She carried herself confidently and must have been the perfect *Ying* to the Major's *Yang*.

I returned the greeting respectfully and asked softly, growing uncomfortable in the unfamiliar surrounding, if the Major was at home? Before she could answer I heard him from the other room, "Come on in Bob, he said firmly, pulled something out I thought you might be interested in seeing."

I entered respectfully, feeling a bit out of place seeing that I'm more comfortable in dirty construction trailers and dim-lit bars then tidy little apartments. His wife followed me into their ambiguous living room, pretty much as you'd expect for a retired couple on fixed income: family pictures, a few knick-knacks, and a small entertainment center. The Major was sitting on an old rocking chair with a pillow behind his back, the long sleeve sweater on as usual and a couple well-worn photo albums at his feet.

Oh no! I screamed to myself, not two-hours of baby pictures, pictures of grandkids playing soccer, and the endless me-and-the-whoever pictures at every conceivable family gathering known to man!

The Major, ever the keen observer, spoke up, "You said you wanted to meet some of the other members, remember?"

"Oh yeah," I said quickly, not able to hide my relief. "I *sure* did!"

"Well, sit down and I'll introduce you to one of our most prominent members."

He closed the album with care and placed it out of my reach. "When we first met, we were standing at the old trap field, remember? I thought that would be a good place to start and introduce you to Mr. Trap himself, Heath Roberts."

"Okay," I said with an obvious sigh of relief. "I've been wandering about that trap game and even been studying up on it on the internet."

"Ohhh," he said, raising his eyebrows as he leaned back in the rocker and looking me hard in the eye over his reading glasses. He crossed his arms and continued cautiously, "So, tell me son, what exactly have you learned?"

"Not much really," I admitted. "Just that it's played on a trap field that has five positions. Each of the five players uses a shotgun to take turns shooting at the round targets thrown from some machine out in front of them. The five players make up something called a squad, and they shoot at a total of twenty-five targets, one at a time, five from each position."

He laughed. *Really laughed!* "Well," he said still chuckling, "I'll agree with one thing you just said."

"Yeah what's that?" I said defensively.

"You haven't learned much about trap!"

He wiped his eyes of the laughter-induced tears and sat back softly against the pillow. "Have some coffee," he offered as his wife brought in the pot and two heavy white mugs with a college logo embossed on each. As his wife poured the coffee and the steam rose, I watched while he began to get his thoughts together, and I found myself in the very familiar position as the sole recipient of another of the old man's lectures.

"Well, I've wanted to tell you about this man for quite some time. A man I once worked for, worked with, competed against and generally got beat by in trap and (he said reflectively) many, many other things. But I see now that before I can introduce you to him, I will have to enlighten you a bit about a sport he and I loved for almost fifty years."

He began thoughtfully, "First let's agree on a couple of things, trap is a game of sort, though I'd rather we refer to it as *sport*. And *puh-lease*, let's not refer to the participants as players; this is not one of those computer games the kids hammer away at instead of going outside and chasing each other around like they was intended to do." His grammar often slipped but I knew it was never unintentional.

"These are real sporting arms, shooting real loads of one to to one and an eighth ounces of lead, traveling from around 1350 to 1250 feet per second. Shot size for common trap loads was number eight or in the winter we'd load them up with seven and a half's for sixteen-yard singles and doubles while handicap squads beyond twenty yards were almost exclusively shot with a heavy loads of seven and a half's. But you're not ready for any of the technical aspects of the sport yet. Let me just try and introduce you first to the *why*, then we can get back to the *what*, *how* and the most important piece, the *who*, okay?"

I was more than okay with that, because in about two minutes the Major had totally lost me! It was if he was speaking another language.

"During our last few visits, you said you wanted to know more about the men at the club. Is that still true?"

"Sure," I said. "But so far all you've been telling me is about the work, building the clubhouse and laying out the rifle range, archery course and pond. The first day we met, you know when you planted that hat, I didn't know what to think. Before you got there, all that property was to me was just another job site. Now I know something more went on there. I think there is still a lot more you haven't told me too."

"The club," he continued in an authoritative tone, "was about being with other men. Yes some women came occasionally and shot, but mostly it was the men that enjoyed the challenge of sport associated with hunting, shooting, gun dogs and generally just being outside. The club started out with a handful of hunters, make no mistake about it, we were hunters first. The trap, archery, and rifle ranges, as well as any competitions we hosted, were just extensions of the hunting life. But let's focus on trap today."

"We started with a manually loaded electric trap," he continued without breaking. "During your 'In-tensive In-vestigation' did you learn that the name came from the very early days when live birds were released from wooden traps as targets?"

"Yes sir," I answered respectfully. "Mostly pigeons, which is why the targets were sometimes referred to as *clay pigeons*. I read that the tradition of shooters yelling *pull* when they want a target came from back then too when someone had to actually pull a cord to open the crates and release the birds."

"That's right," the Major said, finally taking something I said seriously. "That is right." Well we started with one trap, and it was used very sparingly, usually as a fund-raiser or just before hunting season to get ready for pheasants and grouse. That was before Heath got involved.

"Heath Roberts was one of the original members. He was the high school principal and as such, worked all twelve months unlike the teachers, who got a reprieve during the summer months. Though back then, the pay was so low most of them worked seasonal jobs to make ends meet."

"Oh yeah, I remember Major, you said you worked for him as a teacher. What did you do during the summer?"

The Major, not prepared for the question, grunted and replied a bit gruffly, "Construction Foreman Bob, just like you!"

Ah ha! I thought. No wonder he asked about the developers schedule the other day. That old fox!

"Anyway," he continued. "We all knew Heath went to school at some Ivy League college in the Northeast, but what we didn't know was that he had shot trap at a competitive level. Most of us knew it was an Olympic sport, and some of us had even shot some skeet at the air bases we were stationed at during the war."

"Skeet?" I interrupted.

"Never mind, it's not important, the Major said flatly. We never had room for a skeet field." And with that, the subject was dropped.

The Major, picking up the story, continued, During one of our winter Club meetings, after hunting season of course, Heath told us that he had been called to the state capital to work with a legislator concerning funding for the school and met some guys from another club that wanted to get together during the summer for a trap league. It would be called an industrial league since the guys would form teams with co-workers and friends from the surrounding counties. Just one thing, one trap wasn't going to cut it. Each team member would shoot at fifty targets for score. The top-five scores would be counted and to keep competitive there would be a rolling handicap, up to forty-nine, to get a fifty you'd have to run'em. The league would meet on Tuesday's after work and to make sure everyone had a chance to complete the fifty birds, we would need at least two traps.

"That was the beginning of trap at our club. The industrial league was a success, so we started an intra-club league that shot Saturdays as well. We eventually added two more traps to accommodate Registered shoots as a fund raiser for our club, and so we could set up doubles on one while still shooting singles on the others. We eventually saved enough money from all of the shoots we were running to buy new auto-loading traps, build an air-conditioned club house with kitchen and drive-in storage for the truckloads of targets we now needed. It was all pretty heady stuff."

He reached over and picked up the photo album and said without expression, "Here son, you see Heath there on the left, that's me in the middle and Peatie Miller on the right."

I took the album and watched the Major as he peered outside at the rain. "Where are these guys now?" I asked, expecting to hear that they were dead or living with their children but was not prepared for the Major's painful reply.

"Well, Heath was the man who was mostly responsible for our trap program. That's why we called him Mr. Trap." He hesitated and then started again slowly. "He really has to be given the credit for working with the other Clubs, making sure our traps complied with American Trap Association rules, stepping in to head off any arguments. Yeah for sure, Heath was the man."

I saw in the Major's eyes a respect for someone he obviously regarded as a man in an authoritative role to his subordinate position. He was I remembered, the Major's boss when he taught school, so I asked again, "So Major, where are these two guys today?"

I studied the photo, recognizing the Major's steely blue eyes, noting his broad shoulders and sunburned forearms, and a not-so-fancy pump shotgun held proudly.

"Peatie is gone. Cancer took him about ten years after that photo was taken."

"And Heath," I persisted. "Where is he now?"

The Major turned back toward the window now splattered gently with the late summer rain and then simply said, "Apartment 12B in the East Wing."

"You mean here! I exclaimed. Here? That must be cool having a friend so close?"

The Major, turning slowly back and taking the album from me without asking, shook his head and confessed, "I wish it were so Bob, but you see Mr. Roberts hasn't spoken to me for over twenty-five years."

"Major, what the heck happened?"

"Difference of opinion son, difference of opinion." the old man answered.

There were other photos taken at the club of course, work parties, special events, hero-shots of winning teams, and so forth. But that was the only picture of the Major and Heath Roberts standing together. Looking back at that rainy afternoon, I remember now how worn that page was in contrast to the rest of the album. How could two men with so much in common fall so far apart? And why would the Major want to talk about Heath, a man who he hadn't spoken to for so long? Was it the only way the Major could now express his respect, acknowledge the elder man's contribution to the club and maybe try again to come to grip with a friendship lost forever? I wondered if I would ever really know for sure.

THE HAT

I felt as though I needed to break the tension given the obvious pain and emotion the Major still felt from carrying the responsibility of causing the loss of such a close friend. Sharing that memory cast a dark cloud over our visit that day even as the storm clouds outside began to recede, letting the afternoon sun peek through his curtains and warm my face.

"Major," I whispered quietly in a voice that surprised even me. "What's the story behind that hat you buried out at the Club? Why was it all tore up and stuff? Looked like you dropped it in a combine or something?"

It took a few seconds for the old man to decide whether to answer me or end our visit for the day, but he finally looked up, shook his head thoughtfully, and through a weak smile answered proudly, "That son was a reward for breaking my first fifty."

"Fifty," I repeated trying to encourage the Major to continue. "Fifty what?"

Before he could answer, his wife came into the room in the guise of refilling our coffee mugs, though neither of us had really touched the first. Of course, she had a plate of cookies to set it and the coffee pot next the Major. Leaning heavily onto the arm of his chair, she softly touched the back of his neck letting her hand slip down onto his sagging shoulder to give a little squeeze just before returning to the sanctuary of the kitchen.

At that moment, she dispensed more comfort in that single caress than anyone else could've mustered with a thousand words. As she stood to leave, they exchanged a loving glance, words not necessary or expected by either and I knew this was an old, painful memory and not one that could be easily resolved, or it most assuredly would have been long before now.

"Have a cookie, son," the Major offered. "I don't get them very often. Not supposed to be good for my blood sugar or something. Used to get them all the time when the kids were still at home. Seemed like all the missus did back then was cook and clean." The thought of his kids and the life they had caused an involuntary glance to the bookshelf filled with pictures and his smile and disposition brightened. I took two.

The Major took one cookie and his wife nodded approvingly, he waited as she refilled our cups and sat back gently. So I asked again, "Major, what about the hat?"

He reached slowly down and respectfully pulled the worn, old photo album off the floor and up into his lap. He thumbed through a few pages and then passed the book back to me pointing to a fading photo. What do you know, there he was wearing that hat shot to pieces. He was standing beside someone's 1950s vintage Ford Woody Station Wagon with a huge and somewhat sheepish grin plastered to his much younger face.

"Who shot your hat," I asked? "Did you tick someone off or something?" He allowed himself a little chuckle and I knew he'd be good for at least one more story this afternoon.

"No, no nothing like that," he finally said. "That, son, is *tradition!*"

"Are you serious?" I asked accusingly.

"I told you before that I don't make this stuff up. Heath told us that it was tradition for anyone breaking their first fifty straight at trap during a competition, even our intra-club league, to have their hat shot by the other shooters on the squad. It's sort've a congratulatory thing, ya know?"

"Seems silly doesn't it?" his wife offered from the kitchen.

The Major responded directing his reply towards the voice from the other side of the wall, "No, it's not silly thank you very much madam."

Then, lowering his voice, he turned back to me, "It's like giving the shooter a trophy or memento. Something he will always have to remind him of his accomplishment, only you shoot his hat," he said with a smile, "you get it?"

"I guess," I said still very much puzzled. "But who shot yours?"

"Well, it's like this we were in our second year of the Industrial League while still running our intra-club team shoots on Tuesday nights. We all bought reloaders, shooting vests, shell bags, blinders for our glasses, and more junk than we could keep track of let alone use. But most of us were still shooting our hunting guns at that time. We didn't start buying and trading Trap guns until much later. We were only shooting about 100 targets a week, but we thought we were something else boy!"

"So what's that got to do with your hat getting blown apart?"

The Major looked at me as if he were speaking to some unrepentant child. I could just see him setting that poor wayward student down in his office. Looking down on the victim from across a huge oak desk and lecturing them on the need to apply himself because he was wasting his education and how hard his parents worked to give him this opportunity and wah, wah, wah, wah, wah. Yeah boy, I could see that happening!

"Look here," he said struggling to his feet. "A field gun used for hunting is carried at port-o-arms, you know in front of you like, well like this." He grabbed a broom from the kitchen and unscrewed the handle so he could hold the thing as if he was walking though some cornfield or other. "You see, it's meant to be carried in a way so that it can be brought up quickly and right within the line of sight. And ya see these field guns are mostly bought off the shelf, you know, one size is supposed to fit all, only their one size don't hardly fit nobody."

I wondered if he always let his grammar go a bit way back in the day when he was holding court at the club too.

"They're generally a bit short in pull, to low at the comb and heel, had no rib and then you got to consider the trigger the choke and ..."

His voiced trailed off slowly as he looked into my blank stare.

"And you have got no idea what I'm talking about do you son?"

"Nope!" I answered honestly, "Not a clue!"

"Well, let's keep it simple, a field gun, that is, a gun that is manufactured for hunting is designed to carry and point fast. When compared to purpose-built target guns, they are fairly inexpensive, have pretty tight, fixed chokes, and most importantly, couldn't be easily adjusted to a shooter's size. Most of us just got to know our guns and could make them work on game, but Trap, well that was a different animal altogether.

Trap is shot from the ready position, gun mounted. This leads to all kinds of advantages and some disadvantages to the hunter raised and used to snap-shooting game. He might be prone to lift his head before yanking the trigger or even aim the gun like a rifle on an open target in a trap field, just plum stop the gun causing him to shoot behind the target. Trap guns generally have a more open choke, adjustable stocks, triggers, and even ribs to permit the shooter to mount the gun precisely to their sight picture."

Just that fast, I was lost again. The Major shook his head letting it drop a little to avoid looking me in the eyes. "Have you even *seen* a shotgun?" the Major asked.

"Yeesss, I have seen a shotgun," I said slowly and felt embarrassed at my ignorance. After all, I qualified in the service with an M-16 not a shotgun and oh by the way, I really didn't have much call for a weapon when I spent twelve hours a day on the back of a Cat grooming some runway for those fly-boys!

"Well, do you remember seeing little beads on top?"

"Yes!" I all but shouted. "I do remember the beads!"

"Eureka!" The Major said clasping his hands together. "The boy has seen a shotgun! Well son the beads are mounted to the rib."

"Oooooh," I said. "The riiiiib," still very much lost.

"Never mind," the Major finally said shaking his head again—as he had begun to do with me more often than not—giving up on dispensing any technical knowledge at this meeting. "Back to your original question, when I broke my first fifty straight I was still using my old Savage pump gun that I used to hunt rabbits. I had that old friend since I was a kid. It had a very tight choke that meant I either nailed the target or missed it clean, not much of a pattern from the sixteen-yard line. Man I worked for that first fifty and on my squad that night was Heath, Peatie, Billy Williams, and..."

"Wait," I interrupted, "the guy's name was William Williams?"

"No," the Major said shaking his head, "his name was Billy Williams. William Williams would have been redundant, now wouldn't it?" "And," he continued with some annoyance, "Mr. G. Gordon Goode, Esq." He rolled his eyes and gave a little shimmy in his seat as if to say La-de-da!

"Do you have a photo of this Goode, guy?" I reached for the photo album.

"No!" the Major exclaimed. "I gave strict orders to avoid ever taking pictures of that ambulance chasing son of a..."

"Do you boys want any more cookies?" The Major's wife conveniently called from the other side of the wall absent our discussion, but not really, if you know what I mean.

"No thanks dear," the Major replied as sweetly as he could, her chastening complete.

"Well, anyway," the Major re-adjusted himself and leaned forward to be sure I got it all, "his highness, Mr. Goode was kicking everyone's butt except Heath, which drove him crazy!" I could see the Major's competitive juices were coming alive. "I was always a target or two behind, and he had a habit of waiting until we walked to the scorer's table with everyone standing around, and I'd know I had to endure that high pitched voice asking, 'so Major, how'd you do tonight?' I would dutifully answer, and he'd give his score uninvited of course and never missing more than a bird or two. During the first year of our league, he broke two fifties and this year he had several forty-nines that could easily gone fifty straight. I swear it was all due to having no blood in his veins or nerves in what should've been a backbone!

"Well one night the wind was calm and I got a couple of lucky pulls on Station 1, nailed the hard rights from Station 5 and finally kept my dad-burned head down on all the straight-aways and there it was my first fifty! Course, Ol' Mr. Goode tried to leave without his usual routine of asking for my score. That old crow just walked right past the scorers table toward his car when Peaty grabbed my hat and threw it into the trap field. Next thing I know about a dozen guns cut loose peppering my favorite hat!"

We laughed. It was good to hear the Major laugh.

"The missus sure gave me what-for when I got home and showed her that poor hat."

"Grown men," I heard from the kitchen. "Acting like a bunch of teenagers."

The Major just grinned and held a finger to his lips as he stuck two cookies into his sweater pocket.

PERSPECTIVE

———◦●◦———

I have to admit the Major's last story about his first fifty and the hat being shot up kept me entertained for weeks. I tried to stop over the following Sunday but learned that he was at his son's for an extended visit. Then work got the best of me, and it wasn't until mid-October that we were able to hook up again.

It was warm for October, sunny and calm and a forecast that offered more of the same for the upcoming week. I found the Major by the fountain in his favorite chair with a pillow behind his back and in place of the ice cold lemonade I've grown accustomed to, the Major had a badly battered thermos, presumably filled with his wife's ever present coffee. He was wearing a heavy wool sweater, ash-grey color and tattered to the point that I wondered how it could be laundered without disintegrating! The ratty fabric was unraveling at the cuffs, the once tight collar now drooped beyond recovery, and it had a variety of holes randomly dispersed over the entire garment varying in size from that of a pea to the size of a golf ball!

His trousers were not quite as bad; though they seemed a bit heavy for the day and showed deep wear at the knees and pockets with the cuffs frayed and uneven. He had on old leather boots, laced all the way up, and tied tight. All in all, his attire presented a pretty disparaging look to this distinguished elderly gentlemen.

"Major," I said in way of greeting, "if I knew you were down on your luck, I would've stopped at Walmart and bought you a sweatshirt!"

"How ya been son? Haven't seen you for a while." The Major looked up with a forced smile.

He looked tired or down or something. I couldn't get a handle on it at first so I tried to lighten his mood a little. "So," I said as I took my usual place, "how's your son and the grandkids?"

My query had the desired results and his smile broadened as he answered quietly, "Just fine, everyone is doing just fine, thanks for asking."

His voice trailed off and I wasn't sure I really wanted to stay, his melancholy made me uneasy. We sat for a few minutes with the gurgling fountain the only break in the silence so I thought to myself, I'll pass some small talk to be polite and get over to the roadhouse for some wings and see if the Eagles can beat the point spread for a change.

"So how do ya like this weather?" I offered up absent any real sincerity and before my off-hand remark was out of my mouth a Blue jay swooped over our heads and squawked loudly.

The Major laughed and thoughtfully answered, "The weather is great! A real Bluebird day and I hate it!"

"Yeah it sure is." I started to reply mechanically, "It's been real ni... What?" I stopped mid-sentence a bit bewildered. "I don't think I got that Major?"

"It's to darn warm for October. I want to wake up to frost on the ground, overcast skies and a cool breeze that makes your nose run!"

"Ooooooh," I said slowly. "You want November."

"Ha!" He exclaimed. "That's exactly what the missus says too so I guess it's gotta be true, haint son? Always happens to me this time of year. Just can't wait to get out there or at least I use to anyway."

I adjusted myself in my seat now that it looked as though I'd stay for a while. There was a second mug by the thermos so I helped myself to the coffee.

The Major closed his eyes, took a long toke on the moist autumn air, and softly said, "Boy this is still tough to take!"

It was the first time I ever heard him come close to complaining. "What do you mean?" I asked expecting some critical news about his health or the health of someone close to him at the very least.

"Its hunting season son and here I sit! All dressed up and no place to go!"

"Is that's all?" I said thoughtlessly.

"Is that all?" The Major repeated with indignation. "*Is that all?*" he said again now sitting up straight, and glaring at me with a look I've seen in bars just before some guy takes a swing at me. He continued to stare at me for a few more seconds and then slowly relaxing the tension in his clinched jaw he whispered, "Sorry Bob, I forget that you haven't had the privilege of a hunting heritage like me and my friends."

"Heritage?"

"Sure, that's exactly what it was and in most places still is. And you know on days like this," he said sweeping his hand around in a long semi-circle, "Man, oh man! I miss it so bad it hurts!"

"I guess I just don't see the inheritance part of it," I said flatly.

The Major looked up at the trees, took another deep breath of the warm air and began slowly, "We were so blessed in this country by generations of Americans from John Muir to Theodore Roosevelt to millions of not-so- famous men and women who gave of their time, their property and their monies, so we would have places to go afield and hunt. These lands, Local, State, and Federal lands are scattered in parcels as small as 100 acres to tracks measured by the square mile. They provide habitat for thousands of species, not just the handful we hunted. Our heritage, *my* heritage, only now I can no longer enjoy it cause here I sit!"

"Well," I broke in "I never really understood the whole hunting – killing thing. Trap and other shooting sports I understand. Competition is competition, like baseball, football and golf. You practice, build your skill and test it in competition with others. There are rules, officials, winners and losers. But hunting seems to be just mankind trying to reassert itself at the top of the food chain, the alpha-predator—biggest bully on the planet! I mean really, we can get all the food we need from the supermarket. I never could see the point."

During my mindless tirade I hadn't noticed the Major's expression as it turned from self-pity and disappointment to a cold stare. There was a strained silence hanging in the air for a few seconds and then the Major started to speak and stopped short several times before finally, when I guess he had his thoughts in order he began to speak; deliberately and quietly.

"Son this debate has been going on between the non-hunting community and sportsmen for a very long time. Some of what you say is even true depending on the individual hunter. You see," he continued looking down at his worn hunting boots, unlike the sports you mentioned earlier, hunting does not have a referee standing over each participant. It is up to each person to decide how they will approach their sport. Each sportsmen and sportswoman must weigh their desire to collect the game against the level of advantage they are comfortable with. Do they hire a guide to reduce the odds or just save them scouting and ensure access to private lands then process the game for them or do they go it alone and take their chances?

"What sporting arm do they use? Modern rifle with powerful optics or do they carry a primitive arm? Inline with sabot bullet and synthetic propellant with number 209 shotgun primer for certain ignition or do they use a flintlock that may or may not fire depending on a number of variables and loaded with a patched round ball on top of a charge of black powder?

"Should you use a longbow and wooden arrows, a recurve with fiberglass arrows, or compound tackle with carbon arrows or a scoped crossbow loaded with a deadly bolt? Dogs? Do you join a large hunting party to drive game towards each other, spot and stalk or still hunt? Are you a meat hunter or trophy hunter?

"A sportsman never makes light of taking a life whether it is small game, waterfowl, large game, or even dangerous game. It is a life and as hunters we have determined to pursue and take it.

"There are many non-emotional reasons for hunting that can be brought to bear in such a discussion. Efficient game management that ensures healthy habitat by managing the proper balance of game to available food source for a given area, commercial gains for manufactures and retailers as well as hotels and diners. There are hundreds of store owners in small towns all over the US that depend on hunter-dollars to sustain their small economies, but when you baseline the hunt or no-hunt debate it comes down to the ethics of taking a living creature for trophy and meat as sport."

The Major stopped for a moment to take a sip of coffee before continuing, "A hunter goes to the supermarket same as everyone else, but when he sees the frozen turkeys, ducks, and beef steaks, he knows that they didn't start their life in that plastic-covered Styrofoam plate. They were living, breathing creatures, domestic, raised as cash 'crop' for sure but living creatures none the less. Ask a non-hunter where meat comes from, and they will tell you the market. Ask a hunter and he will tell you the animal!

"A hunter keeps alive the independent spirit of our countries founding fathers. A spirit that is slowly being lost a little bit each day. Hunting is learning to stay warm in the cold, cool in the heat, and using your mind and body as the predator we were born to be. It is about being responsible for our actions, respectful for the resource and our fellow hunters who depend on each other to be safe and attentive.

"When you've accepted the responsibility of taking a high-powered rifle afield and use that firearm to collect game you are responsible for the outcome. Whether that is a dead animal to process or a missed shot you have to know where the bullet will stop *before* you pull the trigger. Bullets son, like words can never be taken back.

"So I present you with this paradox, one that you can't understand if all you know of the sport is the 'snuffer-infomercials' shown on TV's various outdoor programming, the most important aspect of hunting is the taking of game and the least important thing about hunting is the taking of game!

"Without the opportunity for collecting game there is no hunt, but the memories of hunting are rarely about the kill. It is more about the scouting, the training, the planning, travel, preparations and people. It is *the hunt* and not *the kill* that sportsman are drawn to. Think about it for a minute, if it were about killing we'd all become jacklighting poachers!

"Being a sportsman is about protecting resources like forests, streams, and lakes that are used by hunters but lead to the proliferation of thousands of other species: animals, birds, fish, flowers, and trees. Even the butterflies and fungi benefit from lands set aside by hunters!"

I sat quietly and felt more like being in church and hearing an evangelist then sitting with the Major in his backyard. Hunting was much more to him than a pastime: it was his passion. It is true that as a non-hunter and non-farmer, I am totally dependent on others for food. Even though I knew of the National Park Service, State and National Forests and so forth, it never occurred to me that the men and women who fought to set them apart were hunters, that the monies used to tax hunters and fishermen were designated to purchase and upkeep many of those same lands or that the benefits from hunting effects all of the nation's citizens. This is not a lesson we ever got in history or civics class while in high school that's for sure!

I helped myself to another cup of coffee and said, "Tell me Major, what was your favorite kind of hunting?"

The Major smiled, leaned back in his chair and offered honestly "Whatever I was hunting that day. I loved it all!" Then as an afterthought he added, "But ya know Bob, if you really pushed me to choose, it would be white-tailed deer with the Johnson brothers up river."

And with that the blue jay cackled, a squirrel barked, and the Major drifted to sleep somewhere, up river with the Johnson Brothers.

TOOLS OF THE TRADE

Still feeling a little guilty about my anti-hunting tirade, I left the Major sleep for a few minutes until the blue jay swooped low and squawked loudly startling him awake. He jumped a little and instinctively reached for something invisible that he must have felt should've been at his side. Regaining his senses, he looked around wide-eyed and asked, "How long was I out?"

"Not long, I said. So, where'd ya go?" I asked casually as I kicked at some dirt beneath my feet.

"Oh, well I was sitting in my old hunting blind waiting for a big buck to walk by, where else would I have gone?" he answered quietly, looking a bit sheepish.

We laughed at each others gigs and after he topped off our coffee cups I told the Major that I actually had tried venison once when I was in high school. A friend had me over for dinner once and his dad was all about me trying some. Said it was the best thing a man could eat. No better in all-the world he promised.

The Major rubbed his eyes, letting the minor revelation sink in a bit and queried with, "Oh yeah? So how'd you like it?"

"Well, to tell you the truth, I found it a bit gamey."

That did it! He sat up straight and almost fell out of his chair turning my way and shot back in that mean growl we take on when you know there might be other ears listening from beyond.

"Ya think," he exclaimed! "I don't know what you had or who prepared it, but assuming it was a wild animal and not pen-raised, it wasn't getting a steady diet of high fat, steroid filled, and synthetic grain out in the woods. If it was wild there are a lot of things that could affect the taste; its age, the sex, the time of year it was taken, how long until it was skinned and processed. All of that can make the meat more gamey.

I always found a younger deer, two-and-a-half to three-and-a-half years old, properly field dressed and brought to the camp quickly for skinning helped to keep it in good taste. Animals that are left hanging overnight un-skinned, even in cold weather are going to be stronger than those brought to the cooler immediately. And a buck in full rut will have a much different taste then a doe taken earlier in the year."

"Wow, I said, I didn't know there was that much to it."

"Son, he said, you don't know half of what you don't know!"

"Well, tell me a little more then. You're the first hunter I've met that seems to have more to say then how big a boom his gun makes. What rifle did you use? Did you ever go outside of this state to hunt? Did you wear that old sweater and those cruddy boots? How many deer did you catch?"

I was firing questions so fast that the old man couldn't even conjure a response! The Major would open his mouth to answer or try to raise a hand in protest and before he could muster a sound I'd have another question shot towards him.

Finally, he waved both of his hands in surrender, "Whoa, whoa, whoa son, slow it down, take a breath man! Try to have some sympathy for an old man. You know for someone who a little bit ago didn't think much of hunting or (he said lowering his voice) hunters, you suddenly have seem to have a pretty keen interest."

"It's pretty obvious I don't have any first hand experience hunting," I admitted. "But I've been around a lot of guys that hunted in school and a few while stationed in Alaska. You know, it's really hard for me to understand what all the excitement is about."

"So, the Major queried who or what is at the bottom of all your opinions about hunting?"

"I went to school with a bunch of guys that were always telling hunting stories about killing game out of season, taking more than the limit and were pretty much all-in-all real jerks."

The Major grit down hard and stared out beyond the little park-like yard we were sitting in, squinting his eyes, and bearing down on his comments, "Like I said before, Bob, some of what you said about hunters was true. Hunting has always had its share of idiots. Fishing has them to. Just like baseball's corked bats, files in pitchers back pockets and the football players that get away with holding, tripping or playing dirty. Sport does not really build character as much as it exposes it or in many cases the lack of it!

"Let's try to answer some of your questions you were firing at me just now," he continued, "first let's get this straight, I was a hunter, primarily birds meaning pheasants, grouse, dove and waterfowl. And of course, I hunted deer every year eventually extending my seasons by using the bow and flintlock rifle to take advantage of the early and late special seasons in our state. My first bird gun was a Savage pump-action, most people thought it was a model 12 Winchester, but it was an old pre-war Savage choked tighter than any gun had a right to be but boy would it do the business!"

He shook his head, and I could tell his mind was flooded with memories of that gun and hunting with it. He took a sip of coffee and started again, "When I returned from the service, I used it for a few more years before graduating first to a model 870 Remington Pump and then to a sweet little Model 1100 Remington Auto-loader shotgun with a Poly-Chock and then finally to my old Browning O/U. I took a lot of birds with those guns. One winter in particular the 1100 accounted for almost all of the meat we had in the house! The car needed a new trany, and I was barely making enough to pay the rent and insurance as it was and I told Edie... yeah I told Edie alright..." he stopped short and smiled and then dismissed it with "sorry son, that's another story for another day."

Again, memories of tough times and family dinners were fighting for his attention so I selfishly broke in, "what did you use for deer?"

"Like a lot of men 'round here, my first rifle was handed down to me from my Father and was a lever action. Mine was an old Marlin chambered in .35 Remington. A great gun for close hunting you know in under a hundred yards or so, but when I began to wander to places that called for a little more oomph,

I picked up a used Winchester Mod. 70 chambered in .30-06. I had others and used them all but always came back to the old 'ought-6' more times than naught.

"One year we had about sixteen inches of snow fall overnight, man you talk about perfect! It was so still and quiet, all you could hear were your footsteps softly pushing through the snow. We were hunting out of a camp belonging to a friend of Curt's and most of the guys took one look at the snow and went back to their bunks! Curt looked at me and said Major; we didn't drive all the way up here to sleep now did we? The only answer he needed was to see me suit-up in my Pennsylvania Tuxedo! He grabbed his old Savage model 99 chambered in .300 Savage and I shouldered that old Winchester. About 10:30 a plump little six-pointer came up over a ridge, and I had my winter meat! What a day!"

"Was that your favorite hunt," I interrupted?

"Favorite, hmm, not sure I'd classify any hunt as the favorite. It's not like other sports you know. Take golf, you remember the shots, the course and the score, so you say favorite course or best score—hunting is not really like that. It's more like, that was great, but next year…it's about anticipation, planning, hoping, and waiting on game that may have other plans! See in golf the course, the holes, the tee box are always there; miss a shot take a mulligan. No mulligan's in hunting mister!"

"Well, I said what about that old sweater?"

"Yeah what about it?" He said, playing as if I was insulting him.

"I mean why do you keep it? Its beat, barely usable and I'll bet your wife has tried to toss it out more then a few times!"

"Ha! You've got her figured out do ya? As a matter of fact, my wife takes very good care of this old sweater. You see when she see's me in it, she remembers the old times too! Son, he continued now with a serious tone, I had to give all my rifles and shotguns away to move here 'cause it's against the rules to have a firearm in the building. I understand that, I don't necessarily agree with it, but I asked to move here, they didn't come looking for me. Now all I have left to remind me of who and what I was, what I really still am down deep, well, I'm wearing them, including this old sweater. I've worn this sweater chasing birds in cool weather over a wool shirt, under my Woolrich hunting coat in cold December deer blinds, used it as a pillow in more than one cold-camp and even wrapped it around a sick dog once until we could get her to a vet. This sweater helps me to remember who I am, what I was and what we did. You see, that's another part of hunting, all the stuff."

"The stuff?" I questioned.

"Yeah, the stuff! Man, the years I drove my wife nuts with stuff. Talking about it, getting it, replacing it, and telling stories about it. All kinds of stuff, clothes, shooting accessories, shells, special rifle loads, oooh son, the sweet smell of oil and leather could send me for my check book faster than a tax collector in April!"

I laughed with the Major trying to share in his delight of stuff, though I still didn't really get it so I had to push a little, "but really Major, do you really need all that stuff?"

"Ho boy," he virtually shouted sitting back in his chair hard enough to rock it and coming perilously close to knocking our coffee cups off the little plastic table between us.

"You really don't know do you?"

"Know what?" I returned defensively.

"It ain't about needin' son, it's about wantin'! Have you ever seen a Cabala's, Gander Mountain or Bass Pro Shop catalog? What do you think keeps them in business? There ain't a single thing in any of those stores that anyone *needs*. The truth is all that's required for hunting is the appropriate sporting arm, a knife, a license, warm clothes, decent footwear and where or when required the legal amount of blaze orange."

"That's it? I said incredulously, really? But what about all that stuff you see advertised in magazines?"

"I know he said, the GPS, binoculars, backpacks, hearing aids, scents, calls, spotting scopes, trail camera's, camo in a thousand variations. It's just stuff! Hunters and fisherman like stuff because stuff makes us feel like were still in the hunt or on the water. Its the stuff that keeps us in the hunt weeks and even months after the season is over, in the sweltering heat of summer, in the midst of a bad cold, when work and responsibility keeps us grinding at our occupations, the stuff is there and reassures us of who we are, friends both here and gone and the places we'd rather be."

"Ooooooo yeah," was all I could muster in reply. "It's about the hunt. Its about the stuff."

Than as an after thought, I shook my head and offered, "You know what Major, I gotta agree with ya on one point there. I really don't know half of what I don't know. But I've sure enjoyed hearing about!"

And just then the Blue jay squawked and the sun peaked out one last time signaling that it was time for me to go. But as usual I take more away then I left. This visit has given me a lot to think about and as usual the Major has made the day a good one.

A ROCK ON A MOUNTAIN

———⟫●⟪———

T he visit was rapidly drawing to a close with the sun barely peaking through the trees. The lengthening shadows made the air chilly for the Major, even with his trusty hunting clothes buttoned tightly around his collar.

"Bob," he said in way of gracefully telling me it was time to call it a day, "sitting around a retirement home with an old man can't be a lot of fun for a single guy your age. Not that I don't appreciate the company, I truly do, but I gotta think you have to have something besides work that you really love to do?"

"Major," I started to answer in a voice that sounded to loud to even me, I caught myself and started again with more respect, "I mean, no sir, not really. My dad left when I was very young and I was never close to my mom or her family. We saw them at Thanksgiving and Christmas, but that was about all the family moments I had growing up. With all the moving around my mom and I had to do to find cheap apartments and working after school and Saturday's I never connected with any of my classmates. I turned eighteen before the end of High School and enlisted in the Army before I graduated. The Army was the best thing that ever happened to me. I was assigned to the Engineers and developed a knack for getting things done. Last year my enlistment was up and it seemed as though I had,

had enough of the Service so I took this job and moved here as soon as I was discharged. Being the foreman here is a lot like being the Sergeant in the Army, its better if I keep to myself and not try to mix with the crew. I've found that some try to take advantage of you if you give them half a chance."

The Major listened, which is one thing I really enjoy most about our conversations, the Major is genuinely interested in what I have to say, even if he doesn't agree with me, he never criticizes or belittles my views. He listens and when he speaks, he is speaking to me, not at me. I never knew a man like this before and something tells me I never will again.

I could see letting the Major in on my family history bothered him a bit so I tried to lighten the mood as I stood to leave, "You never know Major, maybe when I retire I'll try trap or maybe even get someone to take me hunting some place cool like you had 'Up river.' Ya just never know."

"Son," the Major answered, "if I could only tell you how many men I heard say that over the years before they lost their health, their spirit or even lost their life at a far too young of age. If you have any interest in going and doing you should do it or at least start it now."

"Now? You mean right now?" I teased.

Ignoring my gig he continued gaining momentum, "Sure why don't you think about taking a field trip to a Cabala's, Bass Pro Shop, or Gander Mountain? Look around at the stuff—"

Again with the stuff!

"—talk to the sales staff and see if anything stirs an interest."

"Well," I said putting down the suggestion, "there aren't any of those stores real close by, but I'll think about it." Changing the subject I asked off-handedly as I handed him the thermos and turned to leave, "Where exactly did you say 'Up-River' was again?"

The Major pitched forward a bit and whispered, "You know, a real hunter never gives away his secret spots." Then he winked and allowed himself a tired little chuckle shook his head and let his thoughts end in a long pitiful sigh.

Not a second later, he was sitting straight up in his chair. Man, I thought he had some sort of pain or something before I heard him mumbling to himself,

"You know..." he let the words evaporate into the evening air. "Hmmm, maybe, just maybe." The words were delivered slowly through pursed lips so I knew he was hatching some kind of plan in that ancient brain of his.

"You know," he said again. "You know," he repeated, "you just might...ha! Wouldn't that be 'sumpin'!"

When he abandoned proper English and diction, I knew he was concocting something for me to do, "come on Major, now just what are you..."

"Okay, okay," he said waving me to my seat, "here's the deal, I think you might like to visit my old huntin' grounds. It's not real easy to get to, but I've seen that big four-by-four you drive, and I bet you've read a map or two in the Army. I know I could direct you into the church and maybe right down to the pew!"

I had no idea what going to church had to do with my pick-up truck, but I was starting to get interested in maybe seeing someplace besides the club site and this little town for a change. "Okay, Major let's say I'm game, how do I get there?"

"Right!" The Major exclaimed, clapping his hands together as if he just closed a big sale, let's go into the house and I'll pull out the maps."

The Major's wife was in the kitchen and greeted him typically, "It's about time you came inside, you'll catch another cold if your not careful," she scolded. "Get out of those old rags. I have some fresh hot coffee waiting for you. And you need to take your medication." The volume of her voice rising with each word as the Major pushed past.

The Major pretended not to hear and I could see the fire in her eyes ignite. Could be an interesting evening for the Major after I go home! "Have a seat, the Major directed and I will be right back with the maps."

"And get out of those clothes," His wife repeated sending him into his bedroom waving his hands back to her as if to say enough woman, there's man's work to be done!

He returned to the small living room in sweats and slippers carrying an armful of maps and a large road atlas, a compass and a magnifying glass. "What's all this Major," I asked?"

"Well, I said it wasn't easy to find, remember? It's really back in there son, waaaay back! So you said you were in the Army huh? I assume you can read a Topographical map and use a compass?"

"Sure can," I said with confidence. "No problem!"

For the first time since meeting, the Major I felt as if I finally had a foothold in an area that I really was good at and not just a little good either, I took to orienteering like the Major took to breaking clay targets! Bring it on Major!

"Here is my road atlas, a few years old." The Major sorted his documents.

"A few, his wife exclaimed! Really, only a few is it?" She repeated peering over her glasses the way a curt librarian might stare you down for popping your gum, obviously still miffed at the way the Major blew her off when we came inside.

"Okay, maybe more than a few, but it'll still get him there," the Major said defensively raising his voice to be sure she heard.

Never mind her," he said softly, "she was never what you'd call encouraging when the guys and I were planning a trip."

I heard the Major's wife talking under her breath, muttering something about old fools, bug-infested maps, and wasted days on some mountain, and then the bedroom door closed and the TV came on, a bit loudly too, I noticed.

"Okay son," the Major continued opening the map, here put your cup on this corner and hold the other one down for me on your side. Good." The Major seemed to have a routine to this, but to tell the truth the old map was so worn there was no spring left in its folds and the cup was all show.

75

He laid the atlas on top of the old map and started the briefing, as I imagined he had during the war with more than one young Lieutenant. "Now here we are in Delphia, you'll take State Road 375 North to Felsted, pick up Route twenty-four West and when you hit the Sandy River follow it up stream twenty miles. There's a parking area by an old stone bridge. Pull nose in and look to your right and you'll see a big stand of hemlocks. Take your compass reading and move out Northeast up the mountain. You'll see a saddle from the truck, the point on the left we call Final Ridge, cause that's where we broke off to hunt on our own."

The Major was really tired by now, the strong coffee was the only thing keeping him going. He leaned back and slumped a little in his chair as he reached for a nearby pillow to cushion his overworked back. "Think you can find it?" he asked wearily, searching my expression for any sign of reservation.

"Can do Sir," I answered confidently, "piece of cake!" Shoot, I almost clicked my heels and saluted, not that these old sneakers would have made much of snap!

"If you're up to the hike, and I'll warn you here and now son, it is a hike," he said as he took the magnifying glass over the Topo map. "Here is the parking area and here, right here," his finger pointing to a place that had been circled many times with pencil almost to the point of making a very fine hole in the map, "here is where you'll find my rock."

"Your rock?" I said testing his eyes for any indication that he was sending me on a snipe hunt.

"Yes, son, my rock," He replied wistfully. "A place out of the wind, but with enough visibility you could see a deer moving 200 yards in any direction. You'll see red-headed woodpeckers, bluebirds, and if you listen closely this time of year you might even hear a grouse drumming."

The Major began to carefully fold the map as he gave me the final directions, then as an after thought, "Wait a minute, wait a dog-gone minute, there's one more thing that you might want to take with you." And with that he jumped up, stumbling a bit into his bedroom. I heard some muffled conversation with his wife and what I could only guess was various and a sundry contents being pulled from a too-small closet, finally returning to the living room with a battered old knapsack. "Here son, you might as well go prepared. I've hauled this thing up and down more places than I care to remember."

"Great, thanks Major," I said accepting the bag.

"Are you sure you're set Son?" he asked with genuine care.

"Nothing to it." I assured him. He could just nod at this point. He was now totally spent.

The reality of what we were talking about, what I was committing to, what I had to follow through with was settling in on me. The Major really wanted me to go, to see his spot, to walk his path. The Major saw me to the door, we said our goodbyes, and I made sure his wife could here me thanking him for the great coffee. I offered my hand, and the Major took it in both of his hands. "Good luck Son, I'll be here waiting for your report," he said as if I was on a mission to take the darn hill and not just visit it!"

———•◦•———

The following Saturday was cool for the season. I stopped at the contractors shack and picked up a blaze-orange vest and hat since hunting season was open in that area. No telling, I thought to myself, what I'll find up river!

I found the State road to Felsted, but the road was a lot busier than I expected and when I got to the town I found it packed with all sorts of antique and craft stores so I hurried on through to the Sandy River. I turned up stream as the Major had directed, and when the odometer hit twenty miles I found a bridge, but it wasn't the stone bridge I expected, it was concrete, four lanes and according to the overhead signs placed for truckers, it led to a large industrial park.

I found the parking lot and pulled nose first as directed, but it was a lot larger than described: paved and full of all kinds of SUVs lined up like a used car lot. Most of them had car-top carriers with kayaks. Some guides were even there getting their clients suited up for rafting down the busy waterway.

I followed my directions and saw the "saddle" the Major described. I pulled the maps and knapsack out carrying a thermos, first-aid kit, multi-tool, sandwiches, and extra sweater but I have to admit I was feeling a bit overdressed for the hike.

As I headed up the trail, I found it was evenly marked with orange paint on about every tenth tree.

There were families hiking with young children, dogs, and even a girl scout troop for crying out loud!

I managed to get to the saddle where a plaque and bench were placed on the overlook where trash cans and a toilet were waiting for visitors comfort. I took out the topo maps and right there, anxiously feeling the glares from the *Gen Xers* plotted my course to the Major's rock. I could feel their eyes on me as I ducked off the groomed park-like lookout area and dove into the brush. I only hoped no one was calling the State Police to report the sighting of a suspicious looking man, evading normal humans by sneaking away into the deep, dark forest!

It was a lot easier going then I expected nothing much on the ground in way of laurel or underbrush to hold me up. I didn't know much about deer, but I knew there wasn't anything here for them. I found what I thought had to be the rock, reading the well defined contours on the map and the Major's descriptions, I leaned casually back against it feeling it's cool temperature, even in the hot afternoon sun.

Off in the distance I could hear the big semi's gearing down to make the turn onto the bridge. I was glad the Major couldn't make this trip. As I sat and tried to picture it the way the Major had seen it, I kicked some dirt and heard something metallic hit a stone. I reached down to recover what turned out to be an old .30-06 Springfield case. I turned it over and over. Of course a lot of hunters used a .30-06 and hunted this mountain. Heck, I couldn't even be sure I was really at his rock. But still…

I stopped over at the Major's after work the following Monday. He nearly jumped up from his chair when his wife let me in. "Well son, he said expectantly, did you find it okay, was it just like I said it was? Pretty tough wasn't it? Probably still a little stiff aintcha?" he said as he pulled me into the living room.

"Sure was Major, just like you said? Here's your maps, backpack, and compass back. Oh yeah, here's something I found that might belong to you, I found it at your rock. I cleaned it up a little and put it a baggie for you."

I handed him the .30-06 case and that was the first and only time I ever saw the Major speechless. He just looked at me then down at the case turning it over and over in his hands. He tried to form a sentence, but all he could say is "Oh my, oh my word."

Finally, he regained his composure and whispered softly, "So it really is still there son?"

"Yes sir," I said respectfully, "it really is. Just like you said it was and I think I'll go back again someday when I have more time."

"Yes," he said clearly, "someday you'll have to take me there with you."

WINTER LEAGUE

———❧●❧———

The work at the club project was coming to an end and eager buyers were stopping by the model home on a regular basis. All the outside work was pretty much done, and all I had left to do was monitor the sub-contractors: electricians, 'dry-wallers', carpet guys, and carpenters, letting them finish hanging the cabinets and hiding those inevitable little imperfections, which all new houses seem to be blessed with!

So for the first time since my discharge, I finally had a routine with regular hours and time to relax in the evenings. I could get used to this! I was sitting in the local barber shop one Saturday, thumbing through the requisite stack of car and gun magazines and found a flyer for a Trap, Skeet, and Sporting Clays Club about seventy miles North of Delphia. As I read about the amenities and hours of operation the pictures of the guys in shooting vests with guns draped over their shoulders made me think of the Major sitting in that small apartment on his rocker-lounge, pillow behind his back, and photo album at his side. I thought, you know, I bet he just might enjoy getting out for a few hours and visiting this place.

I called the number on the flyer to be sure there was someplace warm the Major could sit and was told that they have a real nice clubhouse. They said they heard about The Club being sold, but didn't know the Major, nevertheless, he and I were welcome to stop by next week during their open shoot hours.

I called the Major and to my surprise he didn't seem real excited about the plan. "You see, Bob," he explained, "if you had to give up steak, would you want to go to a great restaurant known for filet mignon just to watch other people eat? For me shooting trap is not a spectator sport. If I can't be a competitor I'd just as-soon stay away from it completely. I hope you understand."

Regardless of what the Major said, I figured the thought of getting out and around other shooters would gnaw at him. A few days later he proved me right when one afternoon he called and said bluntly, "Let's go! At least it will get me out from under the missus for the day."

I told him to be out front on Saturday at 0800, but I knew he'd be there before that! As soon as I pulled in I could see him standing inside the front door peering out waiting for his *wheel-man* to affect his escape!

I got out and met him and his wife coming down the walk, she walked us to the curb, warning him about staying warm, keeping his hat on, watch the sugar. "And please wear your seatbelt," she implored.

Whew, we both seemed to let out a collective sigh when we finally made it to the safety of the truck. The Major looked over and sorta down at the same time, "I know son, but she puts up with me…"

We laughed as I fired up the big diesel and got us rolling.

We were both pretty quiet during the first half hour or so, and we were making good time, so I pulled off into a small café for coffee and a much needed visit to the facilities, as the Major would say. As I rejoined the Major at a tight booth by the window, I watched his eyes glued to the darkening skies.

"Looks pretty rough, if you'd rather not go today, I understand," I said without looking directly at him.

"Ha!" he said, "this ain't nothing!" He was getting into his customary Club grammar and gruff voice. "We had a winter league too you know. After the lights went up, we shot pretty much year round except for huntin' season."

"Oh?" I asked automatically, knowing the Major would need little encouragement to enlighten me on the subject!

"One spring we used profits we made hosting a few registered trap shoots from the previous year..."

"Registered," I interrupted?

"Yeah, you remember, the guys that pay a bunch of money to shoot at a 100 targets a week and get their name and scores printed in an annual? Remember, we talked about the Nationals. Valhalla, Ohio." Noting my oblivion he continued, shaking his head as he seemed to do a lot with me.

"Never mind, let's just say, they take their scores real serious, love to compete and eat two-dollar hot dogs so we had some money left over after regular expenses and put up lights on the Trap Field so we could shoot year-round.

Well the next winter, after huntin' season of course, we had our first winter league. We'd been shooting trap now for several years and some of us were scoring pretty good (I knew he meant himself), but boy did those targets look different under lights and against a backdrop of barren trees! We started wearing heavy work shirts with vests overtop. Then it got cold, *real cold.* The temperature dipped into the twenties at times and finally it hit dead zero. Then just for good measure, we had a record snowfall in January! But we kept on 'a-shooten' and some of the wives got to thinking that no one in their right mind would be out—in the dark—in the cold just to shoot clay targets! Some of 'em even drove out to make sure the old man was really there and not chasing some flusie at the bar! They'd drive in, look at us shivering in the cold and either laughed or shake their head before turning around to go home. Whatever they had to say could wait till the nut got home! They weren't silly enough to get out of a perfectly warm car! Secretly, I think they were not only amused by our foolishness, they were a bit relieved to. There was a whole lot worse we could have been doing then wasting powder and catching pneumonia!"

We laughed and I paid the tab so we could get back on the road. The sky had lightened up a bit and took some of the chill off the air as well. After we got back on the interstate the Major picked up his thought on his Winter League.

"We had a really good time that first year so we did, but we were pretty uncomfortable sitting in an unheated shed, especially the guy that shot early and had to sign up the others and collect their registration fee and double check the scores. It was after that first Winter League that we got serious about planning the new clubhouse, kitchen, heat, and AC. Boy did that seem a stretch for us at the time!"

The Major finished the trip, looking out the window, obviously lost in the minutia of detail that it took to pull that project off. It was only another forty-five minutes or so until we pulled off the Interstate and onto a couple of State roads.

"Gotta love these GPS units," I said to get the Major back to the present.

"Humph," he said, "I always found a good map and my good sense worked just fine!" With that, I knew I had him back.

Our destination had a professionally painted sign, a staffer at the gate who directed us to the parking area, and a golf cart shuttle to the clubhouse. As soon as we heard the first shotgun report echo back toward us I saw the Major's face light up! He became anxious to get to the field and see the action. There were an even dozen traps, it made me think of the four I tore down at the Major's club, and I felt strangely guilty all of a sudden.

We were transported directly to the clubhouse entrance where a man in a fluorescent orange hat welcomed us and asked if we planned to shoot? "No," I said firmly. "We just came up to watch for a few hours." I nodded towards the Major, who was transfixed on the trap field.

"My name is George, glad to have you here today," he said sincerely. "The clubhouse is open to visitors and shooters alike. Make yourselves at home. You'll find restrooms, our kitchen is in full gear and the shooters supply shop is open for business if you want to check it out."

"Thanks," I replied. "We sure will."

When our host left to help someone he spied struggling with an armload of gear, I took the time to really look around for the first time tried to see what the Major was seeing. "So Major, is this what you expected, I asked without looking at him?"

"Very nice, he said, very nice indeed. How about we get some coffee and see what they have inside?" he suggested.

We were not disappointed. The shop was really a small store stocked full of shotshells, hats and vests in more colors and styles than I ever imagined possible. They had gloves, blinders, cleaning solvents, in short, all the stuff the Major has talked about, only in fabrics that weigh less, stay dryer and cost a whole lot more— as the Major said—then anything he ever had.

We found our way out of the shop and back out on the wrap-around porch. I said offhandedly and mostly to myself, "Kinda makes me a little nervous with all the guns and shooting and all..."

"Are you crazy, Bob?" The Major hissed between his clenched teeth, looking around to be sure no one actually heard me.

"Would you just look and think for a second, puh-lease! They're shooting singles from sixteen yards, every gun, except the one calling for a target is open. They know what they're doing here son. I really appreciate you bringing me out, but let's not insult these guys or make ourselves look dumber then we are, okay?"

I had to visit the facilities again—*love my coffee*—and when I came out the Major was gone. I found George and asked if he had seen the Major, and he pointed down to the far trap house, one that was not being used for the shoot. He said it was kept open for practice and teaching. *Uh oh* I thought, *what is the Major doing now?* A vision flashed before my eyes, I'm standing before the missus and trying to explain how I left him out of my sight for only a few minutes, I swear, he was right there on the porch, honest!

As I watched, I saw someone talking to the Major as they stood by an SUV near the practice field. He pulled a vest and a shotgun out from the open hatch, and I watched as the Major screwed orange plugs into his ears with some effort. To my horror, the young man was helping the Major on with the vest and dumping a few shells into the pockets! This was getting worse by the minute. The Major and his new friend walked out to middle station and when the Major took the shotgun in hand my legs got a little shaky.

The new guy stepped back from the Major and picked up a cord lying on a nearby chair, I was to far away to hear anything, but I saw the Major's torso move as if he coughed and a target flew from the house. I heard the report of the shotgun and the target sailed unscathed. The Major turned to the young man behind him, and I saw he man motion that the shot went high. The Major dropped another shell into the chamber and coughed again. This time the target exploded and the Major, removed the empty shell. The guy with the cord nodded approvingly, and the Major coughed again this time just chipping the target as it moved to his left. He returned the gun to the young man who carried it back to the SUV, removed the borrowed shooting stuff, and started to work his way back to the porch.

The Major stopped and talked to several of the shooters, obviously commenting on their guns, asking about their scores sharing some of the laughs and conversation. I admit I felt a little like the spare tire on my four-wheel drive. I wandered around on my own and tried to pretend to know what was going on but just didn't get it.

Eventually the Major found his way over to me and asked if I was ready to go, which really meant that he was ready. We said some final good-byes delivered a strong handshake in way of thanks to the young man that let the Major shoot and before we knew it, were back on the interstate. The Major was silent for a long time, but finally and without taking his eyes off the road softly said, "Thanks son, I really enjoyed that" and immediately drifted off to sleep.

"You're welcome sir," I whispered to myself. "You are welcome!"

TOM

I opened the lid to the storage compartment between the seats and located a country music CD, appropriate for the Major. I thought we could use a break from the incessant sales crap and right-wing propaganda that permeates the airways late in the afternoon. I found a recording by one of that genre's quiet crooners, slipped it into the trucks system and turned the volume down, where it was just audible. Out of the corner of my eye, I saw the Major's head rock slowly back, catch himself once and then as if given to the inevitable lean on the cold window. When his breathing took on that slow shallow cadence I witnessed a few times by the fountain, I knew he was off in his mind's eye to another trap field standing confidently again with his friends, his beloved O/U balanced in a strong steady hand.

The Major slept most of the way home and when we arrived back at the apartments I pulled the truck as close to the curb as possible to cut the distance of his step down from my three-quarter ton four-by-four. He offered his hand to thank me again, and then leaned heavily on the armrest as he slid gingerly out of the cab. His wife was waiting for him, just inside the large double glass doors with a look that spoke of her relief of having him home safely and her annoyance of having been put through the worry and wait just so he could go off and shoot some dumb clay target. She had the door open two steps before he got there, his head down and feet dragging wearily I don't think he even looked up to greet her until she grabbed hold of his arm with both hands and guided him into the facility and down the brightly lit hallway. I stared intently and watched as he morphed back from and elder trap shooter to an old man. I'm not sure how long I sat there but suddenly realized that the Major and his wife were inside and long out of sight.

———

Phase one of the club site was all but finished so I got busy with wrapping up things with trash haulers, building supply salesmen—no, I was not interested in a golf outing to benefit the local Lions, Kiwanis, or Rotary Club—and the sub-contractors as they each finished their piece of the process. The model home was completed; it was decorated and apparently came ready made with impeccably dressed realtors, sitting at shiny imitation cherry desks waiting for the next big sale. I needed a change of pace—badly!

When Friday finally arrived, I cut out early and pointed the truck south for warmer weather and colder beer. It was just what I needed, a long weekend of sand, surf, and suds!

I had decided to extend my weekend…by about five days, so it was a couple of weeks until I called the Major to see how he was doing. Expecting the Major or his soft spoken wife to answer as they normally did, after five or six rings, I was startled when a strange voice answered. Thinking at first I misdialed I repeated the numbers and was greeted by the Major's son, Tom.

"Oh hi," he said, "I guess you've been away, Dad took a fall last week and got banged up pretty good. Broke his arm and hit his head on the coffee table. The doctors held him for a few days to make sure the arm is mending and the bump on his head wasn't a concussion."

"I, uh, I mean, I hope that this wasn't caused by our visit to the gun Club, or anything," I said. My thoughts running away with fear of liability. What a time we live in: my first thought is of my own skin not the Major's!

"No, his son replied matter-of-factly, he had a great time. Called me the next day and told me all about it. I hadn't heard him that excited since he moved here. Thanks a lot! My sister and I really appreciate you taking him out there."

I spent about a half-hour on the phone with Tom. He said his Dad was getting out of the hospital in a few days and that it would be alright if I stopped around. I suggested Sunday around 1 p.m. to which Tom laughed and said, "Okay then, your usual time it is!"

Over the next few days I wondered if I should bring something; flowers—not happening, a card—get real, cookies—the missus would strangle me, so there it is and why I showed up with nothing but a stupid grin on my face.

Tom answered the door of the apartment and offered his hand: a strong grip, but hands that saw more time behind a keyboard than grappling with hand tools. "Come on in, he said softly, Dad is taking a nap and my wife Joan took Mom out for groceries. We're planning to go home tomorrow but want to be sure they have what they need for a week or so until we can get back."

"Oh, yeah, I understand, I lied. I'm pretty close too you know, so if anything comes up suddenly and he, I mean they need any help or... Well anyway, I'll just leave my card with you. I have my cell phone twenty-four-seven and can always be reached."

"Thanks," he said. "The folks at the church and the staff here at the Village are pretty good about helping out, but I'll keep your card just in case."

Caught up in our own conversation we hadn't noticed that the Major had come out of the bedroom and was leaning against the door to his room. "Dad!" Tom called suddenly as he jumped up out of his chair. You shouldn't be up." Tom quickly covered the short distance to his dad and immediately took hold of the old mans good arm as means of support.

"Major, I offered lamely, I am sorry if I woke you."

"You two guys need to sit down and relax, I'm a little nicked up, that's all, no big deal. Stupid medicine made me dizzy and down I went. Tom, is the coffee hot?"

"Yeah, but Mom said..."

"Tom, do you see your Mother? Good, now let's have some coffee and a cookie."

Tom did what his Dad asked, as I am sure he was brought up to do. Turning to me the Major said, "Glad you stopped by, I really wanted you to meet Tom. He was my number one hunting and fishing buddy for almost twenty years."

Tom returned with coffee and cookies for all of us and watched as his dad took two. Tom gave him a look I swear came right from the Major's wife and the Major ignored it in exactly the same way!

"I started to take Tom out with me as soon as he could walk, The Major opened. Heck I even took him hunting once before he could walk! Armful of boy in one hand and a little .22/ .410 Over-Under Shotgun in the other! We didn't shoot anything that day but it was a start."

The Major and Tom exchanged a glance that said it all, years of outings, successful and otherwise. Memories that could be spoken but never really shared. I can't say I was jealous, envious for sure, but they were neither boastful nor elitist so I did not feel uncomfortable and took the opportunity to gain a new perspective into this man I barely knew. "So, Tom, I guess your dad had you shooting and hunting all your life?"

"Yeah, pretty much," he said. "Up and till about the time I got to High School. That's when it became, football, cars, and girls—"

"But not necessarily in that order!" The Major broke in.

We all laughed at Tom's expense. "I never even held a gun until I got to basic, I interjected, Isn't it kinda dangerous to have guns in the house with kids?" The Major slowly put his coffee down, purposely finished chewing his cookie, and then I noticed that Tom suddenly took great interest in something outside the window.

"Son, having kids is a big decision and commitment."

Uh oh, I stepped in it again, I said to myself, now locked into the Major's glare.

"When you bring a child into this world a parent has to determine how and what that child is going to learn. The first four to eight years are critical to their development and a conscious effort must be made to get their attention."

"Yeah, but what does that have to do with having guns in the house and the kid's safety?" I asked again. Tom got up, and without looking at his dad and me, collected our half-empty coffee cups and decided it would be a good time to do the dishes.

The Major continued, "Guns are not toys, hunting and shooting are not games, but a child doesn't understand that at first, they have to be taught."

"Yeah, I got that. But, yet and still, what does that have to do with keeping guns in a house with small children?" I challenged.

"You have access to the Internet don't you?" The Major began again.

"Of course I do," I answered matter-of-factly.

"Well, take some time and check out the National Safety Administration's webpage. They list all the causes of accidental injury and death nationwide and do you know what you will find? I'll tell you what you'll find. You'll find that guns are way down the list of causes below skateboards, bicycles, skis, and all kinds of other stuff.

Guns are machines. If you had a child in your home, and you had a circular saw or table grinder on hand would you leave the door to the workshop unlocked and the power to the equipment on? Of course not! Would you want to teach the child how to use the tools safely? Of course you would. So it is with guns."

"So what were your rules?" I queried.

"Pretty simple really," he said as he listed them from memory. "One, guns are only handled by the child when a parent hands them to them. Two, no one ever accepts a gun from anyone else without first having them show that it's empty. Three, treat all guns as if they were loaded and never point a gun at anything that you do not intend to shoot. Never! Four, guns are locked separately from ammunition that is also locked."

Tom, having run out of dishes to wash, had moved quietly into the bedroom and was checking messages via his cell phone. The Major leaned over and whispered, "Don't take it personal son, Tom's wife forbids him to have any guns in the house. He can't even take his boys to the range to plink! Her folks are the liberal types, all guns are evil, you know? Fortunately, my daughter married a man whose people were farmers and grew up with hunting so all my guns went to them. I think it really hurts Tom that he can't have his old .22 and single barrel 20 gauge around let alone pass it down to his kids. It kinda hurts me a little too."

"I see Major, I see," was about all I had to offer, but I saw the disappointment in both of their eyes lingering long after their wives returned and scolded them for eating the cookies.

Marriage, like life itself is full of compromise.

THE AUCTION

———⟫●⟪———

Fortunately, the doctors finally got the Major's meds right and he mended quickly. I stopped around a few times over the next few weeks, even took some groceries over. The Major's wife was genuinely grateful since it was the Major who did most of the driving, and she was clearly uncomfortable behind the wheel of that old blue boat-of-a-car!

The Christmas shopping season was coming on fast with Thanksgiving only two weeks away. With the long weekend came another opportunity for sun and suds some place warm. I was surfing the net half-heartily looking for beach deals when my blackberry almost vibrated off the desk. I caught it (though for a spilt second I was tempted to let it go and see how far it'd bounce off the carpet), it was the Major.

"Whatchaupta, son?" His usual greeting when he wanted to ask me something.

"Planning my Thanksgiving escape, I replied flatly. You and your wife going to one of your kids for a feast?"

"Yup, this year it's the daughters turn to grin and bear us! Deer season has been good to her husband and his family, and I'm looking forward to some venison steaks, dried venison gravy over toast, venison bologna and venison stew!"

"I sure hope someone remembers the turkey and stuffing," I said teasing the old man. "No really, I continued only half attentive to the conversation as I scrolled through my never ending e-mails. It sounds great. I'm sure you'll have a super good time."

There was an unusual pause, something I've grown to recognize as a *red-flag* over the time I've been visiting the Major. There's always a very distinct little pause either right before he begins a lecture of asks me something profound. Besides, the Major isn't someone who'll just call and pass the time of day, regardless of the season.

"Okay, Major, what's really on your mind" I demanded.

"Well, Bob, I have a favor to ask, he offered seriously. If it doesn't suit, you just let me know, but I thought I'd ask and see if you were going to be around and..."

"Major, I said cutting him off abruptly, what do you want?"

"Well, he began again, clearing his throat apparently feeling some explanation was in order. I had a friend named Curt Lauver. I knew Curt a long time and well, Curt is gone now and his kids are having an auction. I thought I'd stop by and see the family and Curt's widow Mildred. It's just that with the meds the doc has me on, I can't drive for a while and it's too far for the missus. I'd ask Tom, but he's already lost a lot of time from work after I took my tumble. I'll buy the gas and try not to take up your whole day. Whatcha think, Son? You available Saturday?"

Ho boy, I really know how to step in it! Old people stuff complete with widow and grieving kids! Just what I want to do before a long weekend, watch a bunch

A S P O R T S M A N ' S   L I F E

of retirees and would-be antique dealers squabble over cardboard boxes filled with knick-knacks and rusty tools. Whatever, a promise is a promise. "Sure Major, just tell me when to pick you up, then point me in the right direction."

I picked the Major up the Saturday before Thanksgiving at the retirement home. He was waiting inside the entrance and came out to the truck as soon as I pulled into the lot. He seemed pretty anxious. I was a bit anxious too. I was worried that this might lead to a repeat of what happened after our last excursion to the trap range.

He climbed into the cab, with noticeable difficulty, but grabbed the overhead handle and willed himself into the seat. With a nod and a grunt, he looked over at me and panted, "Well, you gonna sit there just idling this brute or are you gonna drive?" *It was more of a command then a question.* I threw it into drive and off we went.

It was only about thirty minutes down the interstate but with noticeably heaver traffic due to the up coming holiday, and when I mentioned it to the Major in way of trying to make small talk all I got in return was another nod and more grunts. It was shaping up to be a very long day!

We reached the exit the Major had given me and then he began directing me one turn at a time first down one little state road and then another until we were winding our way through a tiny little town that

99

Fifty years ago would've been called a village. Two or three streets running parallel, one traffic light, and a few four-way stops. We turned down the last of the state roads and onto the town square past the requisite three churches separated of course by their common faith, a bar and two volunteer firehouses—always has to be at least two. Otherwise how can they have a softball league! We turned up main street past the hardware store and pharmacy then North onto a two lane road leading out of town. It was smooth macadam with a pronounced center pitch to funnel the rain into the culverts. The civil engineer in me was impressed with the design and the absence of ruts indicated that it didn't see many big rigs.

The Major guided me through that town as if he'd been there many times, and we found the red-brick ranch without a miss-step. It was complete with one car garage, red-and-white metal shed—rusting dutifully at every joint and bolt hole—in the rear and a green colored glass-ball on ceramic pedestal in the front flower garden to reflect the sunlight on hot summer days. A flag pole in the center of the yard complete with the stars and stripes atop a second Marine Corp flag. Both flags waved gently in the cool autumn breeze. The back yard, probably a good half-acre lot, was shaded by several apple trees and an old Oak holding the remnants of a dilapidated tree house whose roof was gone and all that remained was the rotting frame work, which was far past any use, but which must have been well built to be holding on this long.

The street was lined with vehicles as any well advertised auction would be. The auction was under way with the predicted cardboard boxes filled with aluminum pots and pans, Mason jars for canning and various spoons, spatulas, ladles, and kitchenware of all kinds: all immaculately clean and well cared for.

The buyers seemed pleased as they filed by me loaded down with their treasures. As the Auctioneer began to present some knick-knacks—*I knew it!*—and as a family of successful bidders struggled by me pulling a Western Flyer wagon loaded with dishes, I suddenly realized that I had lost track of the Major. Scanning the crowd for that ancient head, I finally spied him at the cashier's trailer completing the sign-in process to receive a bidder's number. I didn't expect that, but hey, no big deal, *I had the truck after all*, I chuckled to myself. I knew the Major and his wife didn't have a lot of room in that tiny apartment and really didn't need anything I saw laid out here. So I really didn't give it a second thought. You go to an auction, you get a number.

"Okay, I challenged, when the Major rejoined me, what's up?"

"What do you mean?" he tried to answer slyly, looking away to avoid my glare.

"You know perfectly well what I mean. Why are we really here? C'mon Major, the least you can do is bring me in on it."

"Look, like I said the other day, I just thought..."

He stopped abruptly as an elderly woman approached slowly; reaching for the Major gently (one arm still left in a sling from his fall) without ever slowing until she was just inches from his side. With his old liver-spotted hand shaking noticeably, he removed his hat and they just stood there for several long moments sharing the loss of a friend and husband. Finally, I heard him whisper "Mildred, I'm so sorry."

"Johnny," she replied as she laid her head on his chest. *Johnny? Johnny!* His name is Johnny! Okay, I thought to myself, get a grip. But *Johnny* for crying out loud. I didn't know that! They stayed in that semi-embrace long enough to make me uncomfortable and then he caught my eye, gently patted his friend on the back and introduced me.

"So, Mildred said warmly, you're the young man Edie and the Major have told me so much about?"

Whew! What a relief! I thought maybe the Major, I mean the way they were, well ya know, they were looking pretty darn chummy there for a while. I mean...whew!

"Excuse us for a few minutes Son," the Major said apologetically.

"Okay, yeah, sure, I'll get a cup of coffee," I replied though I doubt either of them heard me.

I poked around picking up the odd tool or other out of curiosity and boredom. I had no use for anymore hand tools, really just people watching more than anything. This was the usual collection of auction hounds, picker wannabe's, and recently retired empty nesters trying to fill a long weekend. There were small children getting fussy at the expense of young hard-luck parents looking for anything they could use or turn a small profit by passing something along at next summer's yard sale. These are the not-so-middle class living at more towards lower middle class folks. Lower education, lower income, lower prospects trying to make due and make a life the best way they know how. They come for clothes or used appliances or frankly anything better than what they have now and can afford. For some of these people, Walmart is an extravagance!

The Major found me again and was trying to act as though nothing ever happened. "How's the coffee" he asked brightly?

"Pretty good, at least it's hot" I replied as we watched the auctioneer with his never ending parade of boxes and odds and ends. "How's your legs holding up Major" I asked genuinely concerned?

"Okay, not great, but okay for a cold, damp day" he advised honestly.

"So you ready to go?"

"In a few minutes, there's something coming up I'm interested in."

The auctioneer was doing a good job mixing the items to ensure he kept the crowd's attention: a set of wood chisels, a lady's handbag, a cookie jar then a box of toys. Finally the auctioneer announced that the next several items would be hunting stuff, and I saw the Major stiffen visibly.

First out was an old Woolrich hunting coat. The Major just shook his head when it went for ten dollars. The next few items went pretty quickly: a recurve bow, a dozen fiberglass arrows, and leather over-the-shoulder quiver. The Major smiled obviously remembering his old friend in what must have been the summer of their lives.

Finally, the auctioneer called out the next item, "We have a hunting knife here, looks to be in really good shape, though I can't find any manufacture or trade marks on it."

By the effect it had on the Major I could tell it wasn't just any old knife, this is what brought us here today.

"Is the sheath in good condition?" a voice yelled out.

"Yeah, looks good. Well oiled so there's no dry-rot or anything" was the auctioneer's appraisal.

"To bad it ain't a Buck or a Case XX," the voice in the crowd murmured to their companion much to the Major's delight.

"Yesser," the Major parroted loudly. "Yup, not much value in one of them there home made jobs, that's for sure."

The auctioneer was looking at the knife, turning it over and over and said "Nope, nothing on'er. No markings at all."

The Major clamped his jaw and the muscles in his face flexed menacingly. I could see that the Major was focused.

"The blade looks to be about six inches, full tang. I think they call this a drop-point." the auctioneer continued. Sorta narrow little blade, there's no nicks on the edge though and the hilt is still tight. The handle looks to me to be some kind of bone."

"Antler, you boob," the Major hissed.

"Okay then who'll start the bidding?"The auctioneer shouted passing the knife down to one of the runners who was holding it high over his head. "Here we go, who'll give me Ten dollars, who'll go ten dollars for this here bone handled knife." A hand went up and we were off to the races! "Okay I got ten, how about fifteen, fine fifteen it is." The calls continued and the Major just watched until at last they slowed and the bid was standing at Thirty dollars. The Auctioneer called out, "Thirty going once, thirty going twice, the Major called out "Thirty-five," and I felt all the eyes turning on us.

"I have thirty-five, do I hear forty?"

"Forty!" shouted someone in the crowd.

"I have Forty" the auctioneer announced and before he could finish the Major yelled "Forty-five."

The other voice, hidden by the crowd yelled "Fifty!"

The Major, bore down, "Fifty-five!"

"Sixty," the other voice answering immediately.

I looked over and saw that the Major was running out of steam fast and his legs were beginning to shake a little as much from the excitement as from the cold and fatigue. There was an old galvanized scrub bucket laying close by, so the Major upended it and sat down heavily much to my relief. If he hadn't found that bucket he'd been on the ground!

The auctioneer called out "The bid stands at sixty dollars, do I hear Sixty-five? Sixty going once, Sixty going twice, the Major was out of steam no question.

The Major looked at me and no words were needed.

"Sixty-five!" I yelled, entering the fray.

"Seventy!" was the reply, "seventy-Five!" I offered as forcibly as I could.

There was a break and the unseen voice yelled out, "It ain't worth anymore than that."

"Then let it go! I challenged, I can stand here all day if I need to!" Now I was getting peeved. The Major wanted that knife and I had the credit card that could get it!

"Take it then!" the voice surrendered.

The auctioneer, a little taken aback from the heated exchange stared blankly for a few seconds and finally said, "Okay then, we have seventy-five going once, seventy-five going twice." He paused way to long for my liking, "Sold!" The gavel came down hard and the crowd applauded, though I wasn't really sure exactly why.

I secured the bidders number from the Major and held it high for the scribe to record. As soon as the runner brought the knife over, my frail friend took control. Now that the stress of the fight um, I mean, bid was over and as I waited for the Major to recover enough of his strength to get back to the truck, I just stood there taking it all in, the house, the crowd, the day, and wondered out loud, *Who the heck was that guy who was trying to outbid me?*

The Major, looked up and from the knife he was examining closely and said, "He wasn't bidding against you son. That was personal. I knew it would be. He knew I'd be here and he knew that I wanted it. He was out to keep that knife out of my hands!"

I almost tripped over my own feet as I turned back towards him, "You mean you know that guy?"

"That guy," the Major announced, "was the not-so-honorable G. Gordon Goode, Esq."

"You mean…" I looked first one way then another. "How, I mean why? I mean where?"

"Let's get on the road son," the Major pleaded. "I'm really starting to get cold."

I knew he wasn't just trying to duck the questions so I helped him up and we made our way to the cashier's trailer where the Major insisted on paying for the knife. From his inside coat pocket he pulled a wad of twenty dollar bills and peeled off four crisp new ones without batting an eye! The man was prepared!

We headed toward the truck and I offered to find Mildred for him, but he said that wouldn't be necessary, he and his wife would catch up to her when the kids moved her to the same retirement home they were living.

I found my way back through town, "Always amazes me how much faster it seems to go home then it is to go somewhere new don't you think Major?" I asked breaking a long silence. This time I didn't even get a nod and a grunt. "Okay, Major," I said quietly, "I need to know, why?"

He knew exactly what I meant. "Bob, Curt and I were life-long friends. We hunted together as kids and the antler used for the handle came from the first buck Curt ever shot. Curt's uncle was quite the self-taught craftsman. He made this knife for him from a salvaged file Curt's Dad had been saving for just such an occasion. His parents took the knife down to the local shoe repair guy, a family friend who worked up the sheath to form perfectly and secure. Curt carried this knife on every hunting, fishing and camping trip we ever went on. I don't know how but he smuggled it onto the base when he reported for basic training and then carried it through most of Europe during the war, but that's another story for another day."

"Yeah, so I can see why you would want it, but why did Goode want it?"

"Goode had an eye for gear, good gear and knew homemade or not, this was a very high quality piece of cutlery. He made a practice, even enjoyed taken good stuff from other people, that's probably what made him a successful attorney. Well Curt fell on hard times one winter, and Goode made him an offer, I found out that Curt was considering it and stopped him, shoot It all but came to blows between us! What a hard head! Anyway Ol' G. Gordon wasn't real happy with me, and well that made it all the better as far as I was concerned."

"That's cool Major, but…"

"But what son?" cutting me off as he closed his eyes and let his head roll back against the window.

"But how did Goode know about the auction?"

"Oh that," the Major responded innocently, "Curt's Boy married Goode's daughter… Who do you think was running the auction?"

My lips were moving but no words would form and before I could get the thoughts to come out the Major ended it with; "And that Son, is another story for another day."

BO

———➤●⦅———

It was a few weeks before I could get back to the Major's, the weather turning even colder, and when I did drop by there was no thought of going outside to sit at the fountain. I remembered how cold the Major looked the first day I came here wearing that heavy cardigan even though the thermometer was pushing seventy degrees.

I was met by the Major's wife and dutifully wiped my shoes as she blocked my entrance to the living room. It may be a small apartment, but she would make sure it stayed clean. I wonder how many of he Major's friends were subjected to her steely glare as they entered the back door of their house.

I found the Major looking a bit tired sitting in his small rocker recliner, the knife, safely secured at the auction, was on the shelf at his left. I am sure it will be safely stored before any grandkids visit; but for now, there it sits no more than an arms-length away.

"Hi Major," I sang out sounding a little loud even to myself.

"Hello, Bob," he replied smiling weakly, "have a seat." He pointed me to the only other upholstered chair in the room. "How've ya been? Recovered from the auction yet" he ventured quietly.

"Oh, I've been okay I guess." I returned as the Major's wife brought me a cup a coffee I hadn't been offered. "Anything new going on?" I asked letting the hot coffee cool a bit.

"Naw, just another day" he replied dryly as his eyes gravitated towards the knife and past to the trees that stand about thirty yards from his window.

"So Major, you and Curt, you guys were pretty close huh?" I asked trying to get his attention.

"Curt and Me, close? Oh, you could say that. He and I, well we did some livin', so we did. He was the brother I never had. More often than not he was my conscience too. He kept me from getting to big for my breeches. I can hear him now, 'Major,' he'd drawl out, 'I knew you before you had two nickels to rub together so keep that officer stare-down for someone else!' Shoot, he did more for the guys at the club behind the scenes without even tryin' then any two or three others did on their best days including Heath and me!"

The Major's wife for the first time sat down with us in the small living room, lost in her own memories of Curt Lauer and his wife Mildred. After a few moments of quiet she said, "Dear, do you remember the day Curt brought Bo to the Club?"

"Ho boy, do I!" The Major chuckled and for the first time during this visit brightened noticeably.

"Who was Bo?" I prodded

"More of a what, than a who!" The Major declared. A peek over at the missus confirmed what he already felt, she was giving him that cold watch-your-mouth-mister look and quickly added, "not a bad guy really, just a bit rough when Curt pulled him in."

"Do you have a picture of him?" I asked looking around for the photo album which the Major had safely secured beside him on the floor out of sight.

"Here," he said turning to somewhere in the middle of the big book and turning it around so I could see the pictures, "there on the left, that's him."

He sure was not what I'd imagined to find hanging out at the Club. I knew there were laborers and everything, but all the pictures I had seen the men were dressed pretty cleanly, ironed shirts and pressed pants, but not this guy. He looked as though he had just finished ten hours of hard labor, in the sun. The Major could read my eyes and began to explain before I could even form a comment.

"You see Son, Curt had a little missionary blood in him," he said with obvious respect for his friend. "And," he continued taking the photo album back without asking, "he just saw Bo as another lost soul needin' for someone to give'em a little break. Curt could see right past the dirty fingernails, if you know what I mean.

Bo was livin' in a shack along the creek eating what he could catch, kill or grow. Making ends meet by doing odd jobs. He knocked on Curt's door one day asking if he could paint his fence or anything. Well, Curt was no stranger to hard times. Remember I told you at the auction about the time he almost sold the knife? Curt's dad lost everything in '29, but he paid every single debt off, kept his family together under one roof and fed on a more-or-less regular basis. Yup, Curt's dad was one of my boyhood hero's. Shoot one time ..."

"Major, I interrupted, Bo, you were telling me about Bo asking Curt for work."

"Oh yeah, so I was," the old man said a bit embarrassed with himself, "well yes, you see Bo" he shuddered re-gaining his bearings on the story, "I mean Curt knew how tough, tough can be so he found work, actually invented work for Bo to do around his house and when he ran out of stuff for him to do at his place he brought him out to the Club one night and talked Heath and me into paying him to cut the grass. What no one knew was that Bo really liked to shoot but couldn't afford the three dollars for shells or two dollars for a round of trap.

One night he just appeared on league night at the range carrying a beat up pump 12 gauge he bought used at the hardware store. It looked enough like a worn Winchester Model 12 that made most of us look twice! Well he had enough for shells, but was short of the two dollars to sign up and was getting ready to just wonder off to the mower shed when Curt grabbed my arm. 'Look nobody here wants to clean the head so let Bo do it and give him a free round of trap for payment. C'mon Major you know doggone well that we don't need two dollars to cover the cost of those targets', and then he just stood there between me and the squad that I was holding up.

I looked past Curt at Bo standing off all by himself in oily coveralls while all the other guys came in and out in shooting vests, glasses, hats, and shirts that cost more than Bo would make in a week! If I'm gonna be honest with you, I was really trying to come up with a way to get Curt to forget about it when his excellency Mr. Goode came up and said,

'I hope Major, *that man* is not shooting tonight!'

What the heck! I thought, if it'll tick off G. Gordon then why the hum not? All the nudging I needed to do what was right was Curt's incessant nagging and Goode's squeaky little voice. Yes sir Gordon, I said, he's on Curt and my squad. You ready Bo? I called.

Bo just grinned, standing there with a full box of shotgun shells stuffed into every sagging pocket in his bibs! Man what a sight! There you have it son, thanks to Curt, for the next ten years Bo cut grass, mended the roof, and cleaned the latrine at the Club. All for a free round of trap and a few bucks in his pocket for shells."

The Major stopped to take a sip of coffee and catch his breath before he continued, "I can't say he was ever fully accepted by all the other shooters, but he never complained, criticized or lost his temper, which is a lot more than I can for the rest of us."

"So he stayed ten years?" I said reaching again for the photo album. Funny how knowing a little about someone changes the way you see them, even in old over-exposed pictures. "What happened to him after that?"

The Major smiled. "Well, like I said Curt was a bit of a missionary. He took a real interest in Bo, helped him to learn to read and write, the best we could figure Bo dropped out of school after the eighth grade. See in a one room schoolhouse you either get it or you don't and he was to shy and beat down to even try so he just sorta stopped going. Curt started him slow using small engine manuals and power tool warranties and such. As it turned out he had a real talent for working on small engines, you know the two-stroke variety?"

I nodded still looking down at this hard-times man in the picture, wondering how in the world he was lucky enough to knock on the door of someone like Curt Lauer.

"Besides all those manuals, the Major continued, seems Curt was teaching Bo to read the newspaper. Guess he thought he'd get'em some civics teachin' in there too," he said shaking his head. "One day old Bo discovered" the classifieds that led him to a real job in another town. Bo told us the last day he came out to shoot with us. He said he'd never had the guts to apply and talk to the owner if he hadn't been out there shooting with us. He never thought he was good enough to be with 'proper folk' as he called us. Guess after shooting a few years with us he realized that we were nothing all that special either and got to thinking a little more of himself along the way. I'll tell you something else son," the Major said seriously.

"Yeah, what's that?" I said looking up from the photo?

"Who do you think got the better of the deal?

"What'd mean?"

"I'll tell ya what I mean, he continued, Bo worked long hours at jobs we either didn't want to do or couldn't do, he picked up some life skills thanks to Curt and finally landed a decent job. I heard he started going to church and married a real nice lady. They lived a long and peaceful life in a small cottage that naturally, he built himself. When Bo left we had to raise dues just to pay guys to do all the things he used to do around the Club, mostly just to shoot!"

I looked again at the picture of the man standing alone, looking down at his work boots to self conscious to look into the camera, the worn *County Co-Op* hat and coveralls and wondered to myself as I gently closed the album how many Bo's I've written off over the years due to my petty prejudice?

"Major, I offered standing to leave, I don't know who got the best of the deal, but if it really ticked off Mr. Goode it was probably worth the cost of a free round of trap."

The Major leaned his head back, smiled and let his eye catch a glimpse of the knife he only recently out bid the old adversary for and said, if you only knew son, "if you only knew."

GOLDEN DAYS

———————▶●◀———————

The Major and his wife left the weekend before Thanksgiving for their daughters and stayed for about two weeks. They were planning to come home for a few days to rest before going to Tom's to spend Christmas with him and his family. I really have little to do at the job site and no family to visit during the holidays. Most of the crew had been laid off until Spring when we would have some new ground to work. The developers I worked for had bought the Kauffman farm that adjoined the club property, sealing the deal during the last week of November. Guess I'll have work for a while longer.

I stopped by the Major's place mid-week when I knew they were between visits and found him in good spirits. His friend's rescued knife was no longer sitting on the window sill so maybe he's been able to put that behind him for now. Though, you never really know about these things with the Major.

"Hi Major, I called as his wife let me slip past the entrance and through the tiny kitchenette. How've you been?"

"Been good son, you stayin' out of trouble?"

"As far as you know, Major, I teased in return which made him smile broadly. I see you still have the photo album setting out, what's in the shoe box there setting under it?"

"Oh just some odds and ends I've kept over the years. I used to have a garage and a big storage shed where I had my shotshell reloader and ammo locked up. I kept this stuff tucked away out there you know, pictures, empty rifle cases from deer I'd taken, old deer tags, flies my son had tied, just the little odds and ends that somehow you just can't bring yourself to pitch, just kinda stashed all over the place here and there to keep me company. Not worth anything to anyone else, but little reminders of times, places, friends and family I shared a bit of life with along the way. You know those golden days of life."

"Golden? I questioned. Like the color of a girl's hair or the Fort Knox stuff?"

"Oh, he returned quietly, The Fort Knox variety for sure."

"Really, like what?" I asked peering down at the little grey carton.

"Well let's see," he said casually sliding his reading glasses down his nose and leaning forward in his rocker with feigned effort.

He reminded me of the last JP I was standing in front of waiting to hear how much or how long my latest transgression was going to cost me. I must have spaced out for a few seconds remembering the painful amount of the check I had to write to get out of that last mess when the movement of the Major reaching down with that big paw of his to remove the lid woke me up.

When I see him in that light I am immediately struck with both the size of that hand and what age has made of him compared to the man he must have been in his prime. Powerful muscle replaced with swollen arthritic joints and as usual I had to look away, away from the aged frame and into his sharp unassuming eyes. Those eyes spoke volumes especially when he remembered something he shared with passion.

"Here ya go, Bob," the Major said, tossing a small stone to me.

"What's this?" I asked as I played catch with it for a few moments.

"Well normally I'd have a spent shell or a clutch of feather or fur as a trophy from one of my hunting trips, but it didn't always work out that way. That there little stone came from Brakeford County about four and a half hours west of here. Curt and Billy Williams were hot for Grouse that year. Mind you we had plenty of grouse not far from Delphia but they had to go.

We piled tent, guns, ammo, dog crates, coolers and enough food for a platoon into the back of Curt's truck. We set up at a large pull-off in the National Forest and spent the next four days scratching dogs and playing cards waiting for the rain to slow down enough that we wouldn't drown walking to the truck! And no tent is big enough for three men and two dogs rained in for more than a day, you get the picture?"

"Got it," I confirmed.

"We'd been out over a long weekend but now we had to get home and back to work. That last day, when of course the rain stopped, we packed up and headed home. About an hour into the drive, we stopped so the dogs and we could use the trees (which is about as close to an off-color remark I ever heard the old man make), so I decided to uncase my little side-by-side 20 gauge."

He looked over his glasses at me and said, "It was a Parker you know" as if that was supposed to mean something. But when he saw the unimpressed look on my face he just shook his head and mumbled something about the poor uninitiated something or other and moved quickly on with the narrative.

The Major continued, "This was the first time that weekend I had the gun out of its case so I was half watching the dogs sniff around back in the brush a ways and sorta bringing the gun up now and again to my shoulder just to get the feel of it. Curt was leaning against the side of the pick-up, kicking dirt with his boot, and telling me how late it was gonna be till we got home that night when the dogs bell stopped. Just like that we had a point!

I looked at Curt and he looked at me, well I sorta shrugged, dropped two shells into the shotgun, snapped it closed and moved in slowly angling towards the dogs. After all those days in the tent I'd almost forgot how pretty a point could be. The older dog was honoring the youngster (more blank looks from me—ignored this time) and both locked onto the birds with tails high. When I got to within a few feet of the dogs grouse erupted in four directions at once! I swung one way and then another and then another in just a couple of seconds it was all over and I hadn't even fired a shot!"

"Wow, I said, I can't believe that!"

"Ha! Neither could I," the Major replied. "The dogs were crouched ready to spring out waiting for the fetch command, Curt and Billy just stood there facing each other to avoid looking directly at me, saying something about getting back on the road and making up the time we'd lost and generally just waiting to see how I was going to react, ya know?

It didn't take long, by the time I got the dogs into the crates and calmed down Curt couldn't stand it no more. He was standing up at the front of the truck with Billy waiting for me while I broke down my Parker and calls over, 'One good thing there Major, least you won't have to clean that 'spensive shotgun a-yurs tonight!' Ol' Billy lost it. He laughed so hard he couldn't stand up. I thought he was gonna toss his breakfast! I reached down and picked up a stone and threw at him just as he ducked inside the cab. It hit him on the shoulder and ricocheted into the bed. I felt stupid but that was about all that was said. The next week I headed out to the club for trap league and there that stone was sittin', right on the sign-up table with a big handwritten note beside it that read:

'Reserved for the Major. Keep it handy for the next hunt. Like David of old, you hit more with stone than you do with lead!'

We had a good laugh at the Major's expense, and I returned the stone to the box where it belonged. As his wife came in to refill our ever-present coffee mugs I spied an empty shotshell. A spent Winchester Double X and pulled it out without permission. When I realized what I had done, I was sure glad the Major was smiling when he caught my eye. "So, I asked quickly, what about this here old shell?"

"It was Thanksgiving morning, we were seventeen that year. Curt and me took after pheasants at first light. Best pheasant hunt I ever had! There must have been two feet of snow in the fields and walking was tough but the birds were hold up in the thickets where the snow wasn't so bad. We didn't have dogs so our strategy was always work the fence rows first and then climb in and through the thickest stuff we could find. The air was cold but with no wind it didn't feel bad at all. We each had one bird in the bag and then headed over to the Moore's farm. There was one hollow in particular we wanted to hit before calling it a day. Remember, this is before waterproof brush pants we just put on more of whatever we had and dealt with it.

Anyway, the hollow was right in the middle of sixty acres of corn. The corn was in and we figured that any birds near by would be hunkered down in the hollow out of the weather. Wonders of wonders for once we were right. We came in with the wind in our face so the birds flying away from us couldn't use it to their advantage. We weren't in there two minutes when a rooster got up on Curt's side and he rolled him on the second shot. He hurried over to retrieve his bird without reloading and just as he had got it stuffed into the game bag a second rooster, a very big rooster got up, and by the time I realized Curt was empty. It was high over my head I forced the bead two-feet ahead of the bird and pulled the trigger. That big bird did a somersault, caught itself and then seemed to just fall out of the sky. I ran over to where it had to be but no bird. Curt joined me, and we just stood there looking at each other trying to figure out what happened and then a feather came floating down between us, then another. We followed a trail of feathers that were already stickin' to the snow right to a deep drift. There was a funny indent in the snow, we laughed at the predicament and just as I handed my gun to Curt before diving into the snow after my prize! That bird had taken quite a header, hitting so hard it went almost clear to the ground. All that was left to do was dig'em out, which of course had an immediate effect on those old work gloves, froze'em solid so it did. We were beat so we headed straight for Curt's house since it was the closest. We cleaned the game ate a ton of pot-pie and slept till noon the next day. What a hunt!"

The Major's wife called in to say it was getting late and I took the hint. Starting to stand I saw the old man lean down to return the shotgun shell and stop cold half way up. He looked a little pale and stuck there leaning forward staring into the box.

"Major, I whispered. Are you alright? What is it?"

He didn't answer. He just reached slowly into the box and pulled out a small stub of a candle. He held it there for a few moments, turning it over and around with those large swollen fingers.

"Remember, he began slowly, I once told you that sport doesn't build character so much as it expose's it?"

"Sure," I said noticing that his wife, who had started into the room presumably to hasten the end of our visit, saw what he had in his hand and retreated back to the kitchen leaving her husband with one more memory to share with me.

"Son, the Major started, here is one more Curt Lauver story then I have to get some rest."

Without losing touch with the candle, the Major reached down between the seat cushions and retrieved the sheath knife he bought at the auction that had been hidden at his side. "Like I said before, Curt and me were close, close as brothers really, maybe closer. One winter we decided we were going to go on a serious hunt, like the ones we read about in the hunting magazines written by men like Colonel Townsend Whelan our favorite gun writer. We had canvas backpacks, a leaky pup tent and no idea of what we were getting into. It had been a mild autumn that year so our parents weren't real worried. They were used to our little adventures by now and we were by no means children. You have to remember, that was a different time, especially for young men. You grew up hard and were expected to be responsible at a much earlier age then kids now days."

"Anyway, we got up that mountain on youth and enthusiasm. You know, the one where you found that Ought-six case you brought down to me. We had barely settled on a campsite when a storm hit us, and I mean hit with force. We hiked up way to fast, both of us were wet to the skin from sweat but I was far worse being I was soaked down to my cotton long-johns and old Curt was wearing his woolies. Old mountaineers will tell ya son, cotton kills, and wool, well, wool will keep ya warm even after it gets wet.

"In any event, we should've seen the storm coming and either called off the hunt or made camp earlier, but we were just not paying attention as youngsters are apt to do. To busy seeing how high and how fast we could go that first day out. Well the storm hit with fury, sleet, freezing rain, and wind. Our little tent wouldn't stay up and being soaked to the bone like I was grew seriously hypothermic. Heck, we hadn't even heard of that yet, but Curt took one look at my blue lips and violent shivering and knew it wasn't good. He gave me the driest of the wet clothes then made a tight lean-to with the tent turned against the wind tied between saplings and secured it with rocks. It was just big enough for one so he guided me back into it then gave me this candle to keep me warm. It's all the light and warmth I had that night.

"After he got me settled and made sure the candle was going to stay lit, even if I had had dry matches, which I didn't, I never would've been able to strike them, I was that cold. Curt announced that he was going for help. I tried to argue but my mouth was frozen and only slurred words came out. I was scared, man was I scared. Curt knew it and before he left me there he dug into his pack for this knife, he told me to keep it for him till he got back. He knew how scared I was and he knew, I *knew* how much that knife meant to him.

"He hiked down that mountain without even the light of the moon to guide him, made it out more from feel then sight and came back over six hours later with help from a nearby town. The doc said he probably saved my life. That was the longest night of my life son and right here is what got me through it. Every time I wanted to give up, roll over and cry, the light of this little candle and the touch of this knife kept me going.

That and the faith in a friend I knew would come back for me or die trying."

From the kitchen I heard his wife try to blow her nose quietly even as the Major looked away, far away out the window and back into another time.

"Well Major, I said standing to leave for good this time, I remember hearing something in chapel once when I was in the Army about the greatness of one man giving his life for a friend."

To which the old man softy whispered, "Mathew 15:13 'Greater love has no man than this; that he lay down his life for his friends' it's my life verse son."

"Amen Major, amen."

SMOKE POLES

<M>y last visit with the Major was early December between the Thanksgiving and Christmas Holidays. The Major and his wife were getting ready to visit their son and not long afterword I headed south for sun and suds. I'm never ready to leave warm weather, I had my fill of the cold stuff while stationed in too many extreme climates during my time with the Army Corps of Engineers. Why I couldn't get assigned to one of those tropical island bases is beyond me. I always ended up some place that required daily removing of snow and ice for seven months out of the year. I know what the Major would say to all this, "Waaaa, you want some cheese to go with that wine boy?" He was probably right, but regardless I availed myself of every opportunity to be someplace warm whenever possible. Even if it wasn't really hot, it was still warmer than where I was and that is good enough for me to invest my meager Christmas bonus in a small room by the sea.

After what seemed to me to be a very fast couple of weeks, the bonus money was all but gone and in my line of work when you are *off* the pay is off as well, so I reluctantly turned the pick-up north and headed back to Delphia and back to work. As the interstate turned to the two-lane county road, I wound my way past some pretty large farms with large tracks of winter wheat and feed corn, the corn mostly in and interspersed with the fields were small stands of wood lots with second generation Oaks, Locusts, and Maples. These were generally planted after the lessons of the 1930s Dust Bowl and created to help reduce wind erosion and give the farmer someplace to dump all the rocks tilled up prepping the ground for planting.

Anyway, I was in mental cruise control half thinking about work and half thinking back to the sunny beach I just left when I came around a rather tight bend in the road. I first noticed several muddied trucks and SUV's parked in a field at one of those woodlots and then saw the men. Hard to miss them really, given the blaze orange they were wearing. They all had rifles and as I slowed down for a nosier peek one raised the thing, took aim at an old stump and touched it off. Ca-rack—boom! And then more smoke then I ever saw from a gun in my life spewed out the front of it and some straight up from the breech. At first I thought they must have blown the thing up; but in the rear view, I could see the guy blow down the barrel and another taking aim, so I figured all was well in weird-hunter world so I continued on home.

The next Sunday I hurried over to the Major's and found him in the lobby showing off his new sweater and slippers his grandkids gave him for Christmas. He greeted me with a big hello, genuinely happy to see me.

"I thought you might be back in town, Bob," he said and gave me the quick once-over. "But you know something," he added, "you sure don't look too sunburned for a guy who spent a couple of weeks on the beach."

"Guess not, Major, can't really get much of a tan from neon lights now can you?" A hardy humph was all I got in reply, obviously disapproving of my wasted days.

"Hey, Major, what's up with those guys over Kettle County way?" I started quickly as I let him lead us to his apartment.

"What do you mean?" he returned without looking back as he threw the door open and casually tossed the keys into a small wicker basket on top of the fridge. Having grown accustomed to our visits no special invitation to come in and sit was offered or expected. I've grown quite comfortable in this little apartment and followed him into the living room and took my regular seat waiting respectfully for him to get settled in his rocker recliner.

"Well, I continued, I think they might be poachers hunting over there at some of those big farms, you know near the Delphia exit off the interstate. I thought you said Deer season was over and they were standing around with rifles and I even saw them shooting into a stump. Guess they were getting bored or something huh?"

"Oh yeah?" he said obviously interested in this report.

"Yeah, I was coming home on Monday, and I saw these guys with the rifles and knew they were huntin' cause they had blaze orange hats and vests and stuff. Then one of them raised his rifle and fired, I think he was aiming at an old stump. It sounded more like a small explosion then a gun shot."

As I continued I saw a small smile growing on the old mans face and I knew I was digging myself deeper but couldn't help it. "And another thing, you should have seen the smoke! I thought the gun blew up!"

"Hmm, he said obviously relieved. First off, I never met no poacher that took to wearing blaze orange, even the dumbest ones who were stupid enough to try it in broad daylight. Sounds to me like you ran across some *smoke poles*," he said matter-of-factly.

"What? No, they weren't smoking, I said thinking the Major hadn't been listening to me. They had these rifles and…"

"Puh-lease, stop son your killing me," he said holding up one of those huge paws of his and shaking his head in disbelief. "Smoke-poles is what we used to call Muzzle loading rifles. They've been around forever but have had a real comeback over the past forty years or so. At first they were mainly flintlocks and percussion's loaded with a dose of loose black powder topped off with a patched round lead ball. Now they have all sorts of front-stuffers with weather-tight ignition systems, synthetic powder-pellets and the same bullets a modern center fire would use. Where the flint and percussions were meant for close work, out to about fifty to seventy-five yards or so, these new guns are accurate and effective out to oh, 200 yards or so no matter what the weather conditions are. But they all have that distinctive odorous smoke coming out the front when you touch'er off.

Back in the 60s and 70s the State Fish and Game Departments all over the country got to looking at ways to stretch their hunting seasons and giving more folks a chance to hunt. So our state, like most others with a stable deer population have special 'primitive firearms' season. Ours is just after Christmas and runs a few weeks into January."

"Oh," I said, "Ya mean like the Pennsylvania Long rifle, Davy Crocket, Daniel Boone and all that?" I knew demolition so I knew about black powder. "Wow, they have their own season just for the old rifles? Well, that's cool," I said thinking the subject closed. The Major, rarely impressed by anything I had to offer about hunting stood up slowly and peered out the window for a few minutes.

"Tell me, what do you think about this?" he asked surprising me with his serious tone?

"What do you mean?" I replied, my voice exposing the confusion I was feeling.

"Well some folks, mostly the anti-hunting crowd don't like the idea of primitive firearms like muzzle loaders and bows for hunting. They say they're inhumane."

"Gee, I never really thought about it? I answered honestly. I guess it's just like any other rifle, I mean how big a difference can there be, really?"

I could see the Major turning the thoughts around in his head, wanting as usual to get the words just right. "Well son, a modern rifle firing a computer-controlled manufactured bullet from a perfectly formed metal case with precise priming is pretty sophisticated technology. Add into the equation a balanced rifle with a crisp trigger and modern optics and you have an extremely reliable, accurate and yes, deadly shooting system capable of amazing accuracy at some pretty impressive distances."

"Okay, so what's the big deal?" The issue still wasn't clear to me.

"So, he continued, take the flintlock for example. The shooter measures the loose powder with a volume measure that will never be exactly the same with each loading, pours it down his barrel then stamps a patched round lead ball on top of it. Stamps it mind you with a flexible rod tight enough to bounce that rod off the ball to ensure it is as tight as it can be to get the most pressure when the powder ignites and burns. You ever hear the term 'lock, stock and barrel' Son? We got that from our forefathers that lived by these things. It was the WWII equivalent to saying 'the whole nine yards' when someone said 'lock, stock and barrel', they meant they were all in, that is all she wrote.

Well, once you get that puppy loaded you're still only half-way there. Now if it is a flintlock, you open the frizzen and fill the pan with very fine, usually 4F powder and close it up. When you want to shoot you have to pull the hammer back until it locks in place. If, and I do mean if, all the powder is dry, the course flint is tight and the steel frizzen clean, the thing might just fire, one time. Then you start over. If it doesn't fire, and that is always a possibility, there's a number of things you can do up to and including pulling the bullet out manually with a screw extension made for the rod.

"So there," he said satisfied he covered the subject sufficiently, "that's the life of a flintlock hunter. I'll tell you though, there is a big difference between them and the Modern Inline's. These rifles generally have synthetic stocks, 209 shotgun primers in a tight breech totally impervious to weather and struck with a modern trigger-hammer mechanism. They can take synthetic pellets that replace the loose powder and are so consistently formed the charge is basically the same each time it's loaded. The bullets, shrouded in plastic to keep them from deformation when shot are just as lethal as any bullet fired from a metal cartridge and where the flintlocks and percussions are almost always open sighted affairs the Inline's will take modern optics. Mind you, you still only get one shot per pull of the trigger, but they are very reliable, very accurate and very effective."

The Major, having found his seat again leaned back in the rocker and asked me again, "but that's not what comes in question here for most people, hunters and non-hunters alike. Let's go back to the flintlock rifle or for that matter, let's consider the crossbow, the compound and longbow. All of these are classified as *primitive* sporting arms. They all require the hunter to get closer then they would with a scoped center fire rifle to take the game. Each one has a unique handicap for the hunter. There is as much of a difference between, say the Longbow and the Crossbow as there is between the flintlock and the Inline." Then the Major stopped abruptly and just stared at me.

"So?" I asked.

"So, the Major repeated, what do *you* think?"

This was new; the Major was asking me for my thoughts on a hunting question. He just sat there as I searched his face for some sign of what he expected and got nothing but that grim school-teacher scowl.

I reached back into our previous conversations. I never heard him mention hunting with black powder or bow. I didn't remember seeing any pictures in his photo album with him or any of his friends holding a flintlock or bow. Now I was the one that was trying to get my thoughts in order. Not so much to appease the Major, I had far too much respect for him then to offer a weak condescending opinion in return to an honest question. No, my thoughts were stumbling because it was a subject I had never given any thought to before.

Arrows used for big game hunting I had seen in magazines so I knew they were fixed with lethal, razor sharp tips called *broad heads*. They kill via hemorrhage, the animal bleeds out, but how long does that take? What if the animal is wounded? I guess enough are wounded with center fire rifles to, but is there a difference?

My basic training in the army taught me a little about ballistics, but the lead round ball wasn't going to expand and deliver the same shock as a modern rifle bullet. I had seen pictures taken after Civil War battles in places like Gettysburg, Shiloh, and Antietam and knew they were deadly, but how did they work on game? My mind was spinning and the Major just watched me as I struggled to form my answer.

Finally, I looked back at the Major returning the respect he always afforded me when I demanded an explanation. "Like you've told me in the past sir, hunting is a sport where there are no on-field referees, if a hunter within the law wants to reduce his advantage over the game by using sporting arms that require him to get closer or function with less efficiency so be it, as long as the hunter is responsible and can make a clean humane kill," I offered thoughtfully, "seems to me if that is the motive, to increase the challenge legally and ethically, then I don't see any appreciable difference in the choice of arms."

I waited for the Major's judgment on my opinion. A small smile grew across his face and with a nod of approval he simply said, "I think you got it just right. Now, what do you think about this sweater and slippers my grandkids got me for Christmas? Something else, ain't they?

CLUB CHAMPION

———➤●◀———

Winter seemed to be dragging on like a bad hangover from a to-long- a-night of partying. It was even getting to me with nothing to do outside at the job site. The Kauffman farm was surveyed and lots laid out. I was meeting with prospective suppliers, landscapers and the sub contractors but it really didn't demand a lot of time. For now at least I had a regular schedule, at work by 0800, lunch at noon, gone by 1700, and sat down for dinner by 1730.

One morning I poured over the mail with its usual mix of bid proposals and invitations to play in a charity golf tournament being planned by the Lions, Kiwanis, Rotary, and who knows who else. Those got placed on a separate pile for the sales guys. I think it is a pre-requisite that all sales guys and gals come with a ready-to-play golf game.

Anyway, I was sitting at my desk half awake when one of the attorneys from the firm representing the developers came in. Trust me, when she walks in you could be reviewing the terms required to collect the Irish sweepstakes and you'd notice. Anyway in she came with some agreements and what have you, and after some very pleasant small talk she asked if I wanted to grab lunch. Hmm, give me a few seconds to think this one out!

To be honest, I had seen my attorney friend a few times around the job site, and she was definitely not a prima donna, but still I wouldn't have asked her to any of the dives I frequented. She said she knew a nice place east of Delphia that was on her way back to the office, and I could follow her over. That sounded good to me, so I put the phone on call-forward and grabbed my jacket.

————

We turned east and out of town about five miles to a little place that had been an Inn a hundred years ago. If I had ever past this place before I didn't remember it. In truth, I probably hadn't, since this is the opposite direction of my apartment or the Major's, so I had no reason to venture out this way. I pulled the muddy truck in next to her Beemer and we found our way to the front door. The latest owners had turned it into a sports bar with all local themed stuff hanging on the walls; mostly old baseball gear with a few football trophies mixed about. The hostess met us right at the door and led us to a booth passing the actual bar to our right; it was small, compared to real drinking establishments, oak with brass foot pole and red 1950s vintage swivel stools.

As we squeezed our way between the bar stools and the tables close to them, I stole a glance at the large mirror behind the bar to see how bad my hat-hair looked, and I saw an old picture of a guy holding a shotgun with several trophies set in front of him. My first thought of course was could this be the Major, so I asked the bartender of I could see the picture? He seemed annoyed to have his intense conversation over local politics interrupted, but he retrieved the picture and handed to me to inspect. Even before he handed it to me, I could see it was not the Major, but I was still curious. Based on the age of the man, the cars in the background, the clothes he wore, and the brown sweat-stained fedora so common in he 50s, I guessed his age at about the same or close to the Major. I could see the name on his jacket clearly read B. Stumph.

That Sunday I visited the Major and after the obligatory coffee and weather conversation, how's the grandkids etc. I got around to mentioning the picture and the Inn. The Major just smiled,

"So you had lunch at Shelly's. Do they still have the picked eggs sitting on the bar?"

"I didn't see any picked eggs I said and it isn't called Shelly's anymore it's—"

"Doesn't matter. It'll always be Shelly's to me. Good guy that Shelly. I toasted the birth of each of my kids there with close friends and old Shelly, cotton apron pulled up over that huge belly. Never a nicer guy, I guess that's what made him such a good bartender. His wife kept the jar filled with them eggs and you know one time me and Curt went in there after chasing rabbits in the rain smelling of wet dogs and…"

"Eh Major, I don't mean to interrupt or nothing but I really wanted to ask you about a picture I saw there propped up behind some bottles behind the bar."

"Oh, well okay," he said as he straightened up not used to such an abrupt halt in the middle of a fond memory. "So what's in this picture you saw," he asked flatly. "There's a guy holding a shotgun, and he's standing behind some trophies. Looked like it could be at a trap field what do you think?"

"Let me guess, the man looks lean and mean, no smile and is wearing a brown fedora?" The Major leaned back with a half smile.

"Looks like you nailed him Major, you knew that guy"

"Not real well. Actually forgot about that picture. I only saw it a couple of times when Shelly would move it to get something or someone at the bar asked to see it out of curiosity like you did."

"So who was he Major? Was he one of your friends from the Club?"

"Oh no, that son is a State Champion. He took the sport very seriously. He used to come out on trap nights to keep his hand in it after he retired from real competition. But he never really seemed to enjoy himself. Parked off to one end or other and didn't join in any of the conversation, gun related, or otherwise. He never even got mad if he missed a target or seemed happy when he turned in a really good score, which was most of time. All he really had were differing degrees of frustration. We all sorta pitied the guy."

The Major excused himself to go to the kitchen for coffee and cookies. I noticed he was back on a one-cookie ration but I left that alone. Setting down gingerly the Major continued, "Yes sir, Ol' Burt was something else with that Kriegoff. A perfect match of man and machine that is what it was, some days you'd thought they were joined surgically the way he shot!

I still remember the day I beat him in a sudden death shoot off at one of the Club's summer picnics. Hear son, let me refill your coffee it looks cold."

"You mean you beat the State Champion? You never told me that!"

"First of all, there's a lot I haven't told you and secondly I said he was a *former* State Champion. He was no longer competing and it was in the early years of our league when at the end of each summer we'd have a cook out, you know just get together eat some burgers and shoot a bit. We always have a friendly competition, giving away a couple of boxes of shells to the winner. Just another excuse to get out on the range really.

No one took it to seriously. There were elimination rounds and shoot offs as tie-breakers. Well that year we both came out on top of the preliminary rounds turning in a pair of forty-eights. This shoot-off stuff was old hat for him but I hadn't done it more than once or twice my whole life. Since he was more-or-less the guest I let him choose which station he wanted to start on and he was smart enough to take Station 2. Curt and Heath were standing back there and I saw them shaking their heads as if to say 'oh well this ain't gonna take long'. See he would have Station 2 and then 3, the easiest while even if I started on station 3, I had to survive stations 4 and 5."

"So what?" I interrupted.

"So what? Hard Rights on Station 5 that's what! That same bird on Station 2 was a straight away. Some day son I swear I am gonna get you on a trap range and then you'll see *so what*.

"Anyway he came up there wearing that old Fedora and cradling his beautiful Kreigoff. I stumbled up to the line dropping shells and toting my Model 870 what a sight I must have been and it didn't help having all the guys in the league standing back there watching every move. We both ran our first station and then he dropped his ninth. I hit my ninth and tenth and it was over.

Burt glanced down at his gun to see it was empty, walked over and shook my hand. No smile, no cussing just walked off, broke down his gun and left. Like I said, we sorta pitied the guy."

"You're telling me you felt sorry for a guy that had been a State Champion shooting an expensive gun because he didn't show any emotion?"

"He was a machine. Trained himself to take all the emotion out of his sport. That helped him I'm sure at those high level shoots where you had to run 100 targets just to get into the finals, but in the end he lost his passion for sport, life really. No fun. No joy. Here," he offered, "have another cookie," reveling two more hidden in the pocket of his sweater that mischievous smile growing full across his wrinkled face.

A man of passion I thought, and a man I was growing to admire deeply.

"Major" I said accepting the cookie.

"Speaking of passion, I almost forgot to tell you who I had lunch with the other day, so I did!"

FISHING DERBY

I noticed that my attorney friend found more and more reasons to drop around the job site after our lunch at the inn, and I was *fixenta*, a little Texas lingo from my childhood, ask her out on a real date as soon as I figured out what that was here in Delphia. The weeks were flying by with activity picking up reviewing the request for quotes we needed to send out to perspective sub-contractors and plan what lots to begin with and so forth.

One gloomy Sunday morning, I realized that I hadn't visited the Major in about a month. The stubborn winter was finally on its way out with little hints of spring starting to shoot up heck I'd even seen a Robin or two picking worms outside my office window. Of course with March you never can be sure if you are going to wake up and find a pleasant *April-isk* day or be plunged back into the dullness of weather reminiscent of February.

I found my way back to the Major's apartment and gently knocked on that ambiguous beige door. I stood there for what seemed to me a longer than usual span of time. Thinking that they might be out with friends or at one of their kids houses, I turned quietly to leave and employ plan B, which would be to head over to my second home that was outfitted with a number of large screen TVs and watch college basketball. The neon lights would be a welcome relief from the dull not-so-cold, not-so-warm day. I heard someone on Public Radio once remark that March was designed by the Almighty for folks that don't drink so they'd have an idea what a hangover was like! That about sums this time of year up for me!

I had taken a few steps towards the exit when the door slowly opened and I was greeted by the Major's wife. She greeted me warmly, but with what I perceived to be somewhat of a forced smile. She took my hand in both or hers with a squeeze held longer that I had remembered in past visits. I hoped all was okay as she let me slide past and I found my way into their modest home. My eyes immediately were drawn to the Major who was reclining in his chair, a bright red wool blanket pulled up to his chin.

The Major's wife walked past me and gently touched his shoulder. "Dear, she said, you have company."

"Major, I whispered. If you aren't up to a visit I can come back another time."

"No, no he said righting himself with great effort, his wife retiring to the safety of her kitchen. I'm not sick, just a bit tired and worn down is all. How you been son? You ask that attorney out yet?"

That's the Major, no messing about just get right to the point. "Oh, well I, I mean, we've been having lunch a couple of times each week and just getting to know each other a little bit each time. She works a lot of late nights and weekends. Guess that's why no ones snatched her up yet."

"So?" the Major grunted.

"So Major, she and I don't exactly move in the same circles, you know? We're just taking our time and working things out to see where it goes."

The Major just nodded and then sat there looking through me. An uneasy silence settled in, something I had never experienced there before. I was becoming very uncomfortable and started to plan a quick exit when the Major reached over for his glasses that were sitting on his shiny maple end table. He picked them up gingerly, holding them up to the window to gauge the level of cleanliness as usual and slowly pushed them back onto his nose. He blinked his eyes into focus then he checked his watch. "Oh my, he groaned is it really that late?"

It was 2 p.m.

"I've been laying here since breakfast. What a waste!" He shook himself a bit as I've seen him do in the past reminding me of an old dog stretching as it gets up from a long nap in the sun. He brightened a bit and leaned up far enough to see out his window, "What's it doing outside, son?

"Nothing really just damp and rainy without really raining, you know? Not much good for doing much of anything."

"Maybe, the Major returned as he let himself fall back into the soft chair. But we used to do a lot of stuff this time of year. Hunting season's over and it would be too early for fishing but it was a great time to fiddle about doing the things you had to do for the up coming year. Of course we first had to clean the rifles and shotguns, stow the heavy wool clothes some place out of the way and touch up the duck decoys. Then we could turn our attention back to the Club. A lot of the membership renewals wouldn't come in until after the Christmas and winter oil bills needed to be paid for the clubhouse. That's why we always gave the guys until March to get the checks into us. After that we'd order the first shipment of targets for the summer trap league and stock the pond for opening day."

"Oh yeah, the pond I said, we never really talked much about it. I think you told me once, during that welcome tour you gave me at our first Fountain Meeting that there was trout and bass in there. You mean you had to restock it every year?"

The Major smiled. "The pond was fed by several little springs and kept a good temperature and oxygen level for most of the summer, but it was man-made so there were no native fish of course. When we bought the farm it was just used for irrigation and watering livestock it was never intended as a fish pond just a big hole to hold water the farmer and the animals could get to when they needed it."

"Where I'm from we call them "tanks," I added.

"Yup you got the picture, he replied. Well the first thing we did was to drag the ground around the pond and smooth it out from all the ruts caused by the cattle and rain run-off. We transplanted some wildflowers as close to the edge as we could and let some of the weeds grow up around it to give the fish some cover and also to get insects come around to create a natural food source for them. We dragged the bottom of the pond with chains pulled behind an old wooden rowboat to get as much muck out as we could. We added clean fill to strengthen the original earthen dam and dropped the spillway to increase flow. Man, it was a lot of work. We had the State County Extension officer come in and do some water testing and when he said it was ready we bought some bass, carp, catfish, and each year we'd stock it with trout. We mixed it up pretty good with Browns, Rainbows, and Brookies."

"Sounds really great," I said, though I had never been trout fishing myself.

"Yeah, we'd get together some cold dreary weekend you know like this one, a few weeks before the opening day of trout and put'em in. Then we'd stock again later in the spring just before the Children's fishing derby."

"I had an uncle that would visit once in a while and take me fishing when he could, I offered. We'd catch pumpkin seeds and a few little bass from the tanks near our town. Never kept any, we just walked around those water holes with bobbers and worms. Didn't really matter to me, just to be out kickin' around the water was the best part."

"That was our goal as well. We intentionally set it up so the kids would want to come out and get a little muddy and wet. Maybe they'd catch a couple fish, maybe not but for some of them. This was the only chance they'd have all year to get outside someplace other than the back yard or playground. We must've been doing something right, because each year it just got bigger and bigger. We had people coming out that lived near Delphia that none of us even knew. When the subdivisions started to really kick in, we'd get the new families moving into the area as well. Eventually, we bought an old vinyl swimming pool that we set up in the field and had the town's fire company fill it up. We always kept some really nice fish for the pool and only let the real little kids fish it. Some of them kids couldn't even see over the edge of the three-foot high side! Go ahead," he said pointing to the little book shelf across the room. "Grab the photo album and turn towards the back. There should be a few pictures of some of the fishing derbies in there."

"Wow," I said, scouring the pictures. Some of the shots took in the entire pond lined with kids of every size while others were of junior anglers holding their prize catch, some kids so small the fishtails were touching the grass. "There's a lot of people at some of these outings. How much did you guys pull in from this event?" I blurted out the question without even thinking, and before the last syllable left my big mouth I felt the Major's scour bearing down over those glasses.

"Look here mister, he started with emotion before having to stop to fight back a dry cough I hadn't noticed before. This was pure community service. It was about and for the kids. Not about revenue. Remember what I said, some of these kids would never get out if it wasn't for this event. We collected old rods and reels during the year and the members would tear them down, grease the gears and then make them available for the kids. This wasn't about making money, this was a way to give something back and yes, it was all free of charge. Can you understand that?"

"I guess, but it seems to me that you guys were missing a golden chance to bring in some extra money for your club if it was a popular as it looks."

"*Extra* Money? the Major grunted. I don't know about you son, but I ain't never had any of that kind. Back in the 60s the folks around here, like all over the country was in transition and moving further and further from our agriculture roots. Kids were loosing touch with nature and the outdoors. TV and other stuff were taking them inside instead of being outside chasing butterflies and turning rocks over to find salamanders. Most of em', their parents included had never wetted a line or saw a firearm in real life, let alone talk to a sportsman. We just wanted kids to appreciate catching the fish, and if their mom and dad approved, we'd clean and bag em' so they could take them home and eat them. In one morning of fishing, they got a real object lesson in nature. Some of those little guys went on to be adult fishermen. More than a few grew up and joined our club and a couple we sponsored over the years even went on to get biology degrees. And one more thing, you know what all these kids went on to become?"

"No, Major, what was that?"

"Voters, that's what. Mostly anti's—hunting, fishing, guns whatever is generally due to ignorance. Afraid of something they just don't understand or have never experienced. By taking these kids out and showing them and their parents that we really weren't crazy gun nuts to be feared they might just remember us come election day, and if they didn't become an out-and-out supporter, they might at least not fight against us as we tried to preserve this way of life of ours. So you tell me Son."

"Yes Major?"

"How do you put a price on that?"

This outpouring of emotion really took a lot out of the Major as he leaned back to rest, probably thinking about those days in the damp weather helping kids and their parents at the pond. I thumbed through the rest of the fishing pictures: boys, girls, parents, families, and volunteers—all those club volunteers standing near by looked as happy with the catch as the kids themselves.

I continued to page through the album and wondered where they all were? How much impact could a little thing like taking a kid fishing really make? Then I remembered my uncle Nick who was also a contractor and who encouraged me to pursue the Army Corps of Engineers when I told him I planned to enlist after graduation. That conversation I remembered was during one of those fishing outings he took me on near home while I was still in High School.

I looked back to the album, the black and white photos and then later in glowing color. How many, I wondered to myself, how many *Uncle Nicks* were in them?

The Major had drifted off to sleep. How old he seemed to me now. Not the same man I met last year at the club property coming out to bury that shot-up hat, talking to me about passion, a man who suddenly seemed to me to be a lot like Uncle Nick.

EXPANSION

———◆———

The Major looked really tired and worn the last time I was over at his apartment. After he fell asleep, I slipped out quietly and by the worried look I got from his wife I knew there was more to the Majors condition then just the usual winter SAD malady. I've never been very good at dealing with the elderly or the infirm. A character flaw I'm not proud of but watching people suffer physically has always made me uncomfortable. That was one of the reasons I enlisted and left my own mother in the care of professionals where she spent her last, lost years. By then she didn't know anyone including me, slipping into that abyss they call *Alzheimer's*. She died peacefully while I was in Alaska. I can't really say what I felt when the Chaplin and my LT called me in to break the news. Okay, is all I said and then requested to be dismissed. I never shed a tear and not because I had any issues with her, heck I hardly knew her. Dad was long gone, she worked night and day to keep us fed and pay the rent. I went to school everyday, was working by fourteen, and learned to take care of myself. I'm probably the only guy I know that ate better and more often in the chow hall than I did at home!

I'd been avoiding going to the Major's place, choosing instead to drive north to the State Capital and visit a certain female attorney on the weekends. Let's just say the conversation is rich and holds my attention and leave it at that! Finally and after more weeks had gone by than I realized, one Thursday afternoon my cell vibrated me to attention. It was Tom, the Major's son. "What's up Tom, how's your dad?" My voice friendly but cautious. "He behavin' himself?"

"He's hanging in there…" Tom said and then came the dead-pain reply, "but he's getting pretty weak." There was an awful long pause then he started his plea, "I…um that is…I mean we, Sis and I we were, you know…wondering, hoping really that you could drop around this weekend if it's not to much trouble and see Dad. You wouldn't have to stay very long, just kinda stick your head in and say hi. It'd mean a lot to Dad."

"Sure Tom, I must have said, though my mind was still thinking of ways to bail. Sunday's still good for the Major?"

"Perfect, Tom returned a little brighter, your usual time, One o'clock. We'll let Mom know to expect you."

We both hesitated knowing or at least sensing there was a lot more to say.

"Tom?"

"Yeah?"

"Does he, you know, need anything?"

"Not at the moment. But thanks for asking."

———————

I drove a little slower than normal on my way to the Major's that Sunday and not just because I was a little hung over either, I flat out didn't want to go. In fact I was dreading it, hence the one or two, too many rum and cokes at dinner, and oh my stupid pounding head! I wasn't this nervous coming over last summer for my first visit. Man does that seem like a long time ago.

After parking my *duelly*, taking up double spaces as usual I moved quickly into the lobby and past the greeters who by now recognized me. The regular group of elderly men and one woman, who were on duty that day, avoided looking directly at me as I past. They were however quick to whisper to one another when they thought I was beyond earshot. What the heck did they know that I didn't? Better still, what did they know that I didn't want to know? Down the ammonia smelling hallway I went, forcing myself to pick up the pace and ignore the beige walls and maroonish colored carpet which was blurring before me as I made my way through the place. I hate maroon.

When I looked up, I was standing at the Major's door. I no longer needed to let my eyes follow the line of apartment numbers to guide me to the apartment. I could find this one blindfolded now. I knocked gently and the Major's wife quietly let me in. I'm not used to being around women and have been told by more than one that I am a brainless clod, but it didn't take Dr. Phil to see her red eyes and clump of tissues in her hand to know she was pretty upset. She let me in and smiled as warmly as she had in the past.

I found the Major in his chair though looking now very much the old man I suspect he had rapidly become. I noticed that his mouth drooped involuntarily and sagged open. His eyes were open but had lost most of that twinkle I loved so much when he was up to stealing the forbidden cookies. My stomach tightened noticeably.

"So Major I whispered, you staying out of trouble?"

I placed my hand gently on his arm and was surprised at the thick layers of clothes he was wearing under the heavy sweater that was buttoned to the top. In addition to the layered clothing, he was also partially covered by his favorite red woolen blanket even though with my light jacket pulled off and tossed down onto the carpet beside my regular seat, I was already beginning to sweat in the close quarters.

"Hi Son, he replied, Guess I'm in no danger of getting into any of that at the moment, am I now?"

Ho boy! This is going to be tough! Ignoring his comment I took the two short steps across the room to my well-worn seat and settled lightly, still planning an early escape. He really didn't look too interested in my visit anyway so I figured to make some small talk, probably sip some coffee, and get the heck out of Dodge!

"Well, sir," I opened to break the silence, "I've been pretty busy lately. You know summer's coming and oh yeah not sure you heard but we picked up the Kauffman farm that adjoins the Club property. All the paperwork is done and the farmer's Grandkids are off to buy their new cars and fishing boats. I have the surveyors coming in this week and then the excavators to see what top soil we can sell. Not enough trees on that property to worry with the loggers so we'll just knock down what we have to and offer it up piecemeal"

I'd been rambling almost to myself, really just a canned *mean-nothin'* talk to fill some time before I bolt. Then I noticed the Major looking up and at me for the first time that afternoon.

"The Kauffman farm huh? he grumbled. Well the grandkids had no interest in farming. The old man's boys were too old now to work it even if they wanted too." That seemed to be about it so with a harried humph, he sorta just went limp and I figured that was that.

"So" I started again, as I accepted the predicted cup of coffee from his dear wife. "The old man, the Grandfather I mean, the original Mr. Kauffman was he a member of the club?"

"Ha! the Major stirred to life. That woulda' been the day! He hated the club. He figured he should've had that land instead of us but we beat'em to it. He did everything he could to get in our way. Didn't matter what we were doing. If it happened at, was planned by or put on for the Club, he were agin' it!"

The mischievous chuckle told me that last bit of pathetic English was an inside joke, probably at the now deceased Mr. Kauffman's expense. The Major was wiggling himself back upright in his chair even as he continued. "I remember when we first started the expansion he pulled every trick in the book to get in our way."

"Expansion? You mean more property?" I asked.

"No, I mean we expanded the buildings, the trap field and rifle ranges at the club. We were getting a lot of new members that wanted more stuff to do: black powder, archery, trap leagues, small bore leagues, man it was coming at us so fast! We no sooner got one committee named and a new idea hit us upside the head! Man oh man! Well, old man Kauffman had the township over at his place when we'd shoot trap trying to say we were violating some noise regulation when he knew darn well there was no noise ordinance! Just smoke and mirrors to annoy us. When we cut in the field archery course, he called the township and claimed we broke the law cause we didn't have a commercial logging license, and when we added a kitchen to the clubhouse to sell hot dogs and stuff he called the Department of Health! What nonsense!"

The Major's wife must have sensed an improvement in his disposition and for only the second time during one of my visits, came in and just sat at the little dinner table with a cup of tea. She just sat and listened. Her thoughts were her own. I think maybe, looking back now she just wanted to hear his voice with some life in it again. It was sure starting to sound a lot better to me too.

The Major leaned over and winked. "Ya see son, that old farmer, the one that sold us the club ground, well he was old man Kauffman's cousin Walt Flynn and Kauffman thought that should've been his land. I guess it was a family thing, but Flynn was having none of it. He knew Kauffman would clear all the trees just so he could plant a few hundred more acres of feed corn and soy beans. Flynn loved those trees—loved to hear the wind rustle them in the fall, watched them every spring from tiny buds to broad leafs. No sir, Flynn had to sell but he'd be darned if he'd let Kauffman sell off those trees for timber. Good Ol' Walt Flynn!"

The Major was visibly worn out but you could tell his spirit was revived, at least for the time being. He sat up and leaned back into his chair then asked his wife for some tea. She all but jumped out of her chair to prepare it for him. Alone again, I thought it might be time.

"Major?"

"Yeah?"

"C'mon Major, what's really going on? What's wrong? You got a lot of people worried about you."

The Major obviously agitated by my directness looked past me and out the window, though I knew all he could see was the very tops of the trees. "Son, if you make it this long you'll know. You'll know for sure."

I assumed the door was shut and I started to stand when the Major, taking the hot tea from his wife caught me with a direct question of his own. "What's your boss gonna do with Kauffman's farm house?"

"It's been left go for years, I said as I sat back down. It'd never pass code and besides we can get a couple of new houses on the same plot by moving some of the trees and re-grading. Why?"

"Nothing in particular, just wondering."

"Yeah right, c'mon Major give it up," I teased.

"Well it's just," the Major stopped and looked at me with brightening eyes, "Man, if we could've got hold of that farm back in the day, we'd showed them what a real club could be! Now that woulda been an *expansion*, haint?"

157

"Yeah Major, it would've been something that's for sure. By the way there's someone I want you to meet. Maybe I'll bring her around one of these days. When you're up to it."

"Up to it? You hear this boy Mother? When I'm up to it?"

His wife smiled with eyes filling with tears even as she took sanctuary in her beloved kitchen.

"So you haven't just been avoiding a sick old man. You went and finally asked that attorney friend of yours out, so you did? There's hope for you yet son, there is hope for you yet!"

"Well that Major, is still left to be seen." Then after a breath I caught his gaze and added, "Haint?"

COST OF AMBITION

———————

I called Tom that night and let him know that I visited his dad. We talked a little about the Major in general terms, and then I finally had to ask, "Look Tom, I don't want to pry into family business or anything but what really is the matter with your dad? He isn't looking or acting like the spirited man I met last year."

There was a strained silence and then Tom began slowly, "Early last summer, that'd been a few months before you met Dad, he was diagnosed with, well Dad calls it a 'condition.' You know folks his age really want to keep things private and any more than that will have to come directly from him. I hope you understand?"

"Of course I do. So how long..." which sounded awfully abrupt even to me. So I took a breath, steadied myself, and started again. "I mean Tom, he looked pretty strung out Sunday, can he stand the stress of visitors? Should I go back or just forget about it?"

I waited and though my visit ended okay, I really had no interest in watching whatever it was eat him away slowly. I wanted to remember the Major the way he was, feisty and mischievous. Sneaking off to shoot some targets behind my back, fighting for his friend's knife and stealing cookies right under his wife's nose! That's the man I wanted to remember not an invalid. Not someone like my Mom.

"No, no, you see that's the weird thing. The doctor laid it right out and all but dad should not be this down at this point. His meds are all thought out, and he should be good to go. Don't get me wrong, he's not going to be running up and down the hallway, but he should still be up and around. Slowing down for sure but not stuck in that chair. Sis called the Doc last week, before you went, and they're thinking about treating him for depression. Man! Dad! Depression? No way, not Dad! He's the most positive person I ever knew. There has to be something else. Did he say anything at all that I can tell the doctor?"

"I wish he had," I replied. "I know he perked up there at the end of the visit when he was thinking about the Kauffman farm, and telling me all the stuff about expanding the club. But nothing really we haven't heard before."

"I know this is way out of line," Tom said, the rest of the sentence wasn't necessary.

"Sure Tom, I'd be glad to go back over and I promise to call you as soon as I can and fill you in. Who knows maybe we'll get somewhere this week."

"Yeah," Tom said, "who knows? Well thanks. I don't know how to…"

"You don't have to and please don't try." And with that the phone was silent again.

My female attorney friend had to work the following Sunday, something that wasn't unusual for young professionals in her line of work. Maybe that's why a bright, attractive woman like her was still available and seeing a straggly guy like me with long hair, a big pick up, and dirty boots. Anyway, I found myself driving right back to the Major's again, maybe even more reluctant now that I spoke with Tom than the previous week. I found the same parking spot as last Sunday, slipped past the same greeters who were on duty yet again—I wondered if they really had apartments or just lived there, in the lobby!—down the hall—I still hate maroon!—and marched up to that cold beige door. *Here I go again.*

I knocked softly half-hoping they wouldn't be home, but the Major's wife must have been waiting for me and opened the door before my hand could drop to my side. She let me slip by, and I found the Major right where I left him last week, slumping in that rocker recliner, bundled up beyond belief.

"Hello Major," I called trying to act as *normal* as I could. I hated acting anything but for his sake I'd suffer through it. "Looks like you've grown to liken' that old chair or did the missus lock you out of the bedroom for stealing cookies?"

The Major brightened a bit, looked up squinting, the light above my head hurting his eyes and whispered, "Hello son. Well two weeks in a row. That special person of yours stood you up again I bet and you don't want to drink your own coffee, haint?"

We tried to laugh at each others expense the way we used to do, though I have to admit it seemed to be a bit shallow now in his condition. There didn't appear to be much more to say at the moment. The Major looked past me as I sat down and gave a little sigh. I knew I had to get him talking again. That always seemed to bring him back to his old self. The concern of Tom's voice still rang in my head...*Not Dad, not Dad.*

"So, I ventured, you were filling me in on the expansion." Picking up the conversation where we left off the previous week, I watched as the Major strained to remember our last visit. Inside I was screaming and cheering him on: C'mon Major, you can do it. Dig deep. C'mon dig it out! Don't you quit on me!

"That's right he said, more to himself than to me, that's right. Expansion. Kauffman's farm. Walt Flynn. Expansion, Expansion..."

Something I was doing was working, whether it was working for or against him was yet to be seen, but I started this thing and was going to see it through. "Yes sir," I said, "the expansion out at the club, remember?"

"Well yeah, I remember" he said sitting up as he got his bearings. "That was really the pinnacle of the club years, so it was, at least for us charter members anyway. The first twenty years was all new for us, building rifle ranges, saving for and then buying the traps, forming our leagues, and experimenting with the when and how of stocking the pond. We made some real blunders along the way, but all in all we learned a lot about running a club for sportsman. There were a lot bigger clubs than ours around, but I'd put our leadership and core working members up against any of them for pure dedication and hard work. Yes sir! Those were some days, so they were. We..."

His voice trailed off and you could see his mind's eye was back out there with a memory of something or someone that held him transfixed in time. He glanced at the photo album and then felt for Curt's ever present knife. He began to clinch and loosen his left fist as if he was readying for a fight. For the first time, I realized there was more eating at this man then just some disease. He was being eaten up by something in his past. Something at that club a heck of a lot more serious than a hat shot full of holes that he buried out there, something else buried as it were inside that old man's soul.

"Major," I whispered again, reaching out for his arm. "Major, what happened? Tell me. What happened?" Out of the corner of my eye I saw his wife slip silently into the room and sat at the dinner table, the Major turned towards her longing for her support. She nodded encouragement first to him and then to me, willing me to understand, to be patient and to somehow help him find some peace.

Once again, I reached out to him, "C'mon Major, what is it?"

The old man straightened the best he could to prepare himself for the confession. He cleared his throat and began very slowly "You see at that time everyone was all for expansion. Shoot, it's the American way son. Build it bigger, more expensive, and more expansive, more-bigger-better, that was our motto. We had some money and needed just a little more, it seemed like we or at least *I* always pushed for just a little more. I really wanted a second clubhouse just for the trap shooters, right next to the newly expanded field. Not just a big shed mind you, nothing but the best would do for me mister! I wanted a nice clubhouse. It had to be heated, have big windows, a full kitchen and an office. I went so far as promise that we'd even have AC by George! We were almost there and I was getting anxious to get on with it. We had most of the money we needed, and if we broke ground before the end of May we'd be in it way before fall hunting season.

Heath kept trying to slow the project down, slow me down really. We had some pretty heated though up to this point private conversations over the money. I had all the answers, we'd beg, borrow and sell anything not nailed down if necessary but we were going to have that house!

Finally at the club's second quarterly business meeting that year it all came to a head. I pressured all the guys I knew into supporting me telling them how great the club would be. I stood up there and the manure started flying, I said: 'listen up people, maybe some of you want to stay a little rinky-dink club but we can really do something here.' All my guys started hooting it up, and I yelled even louder, 'not only that, but we can be one of the best clubs in the county,' then I went for it, 'we can be the best darn club in the state!' They all jumped up and cheered and yelled. They were pounding me on my back, pumping my hand congratulating me. Man my head was so big I wonder how I got it through the door when we finally left that night.

"Boy was I worked up but Heath had heard enough. He knew my tirade was pointed at him, and he just slipped out the back. No one even said goodbye to him or nothing. Think of it. The man that I leaned on, the man that worked so hard for that club just let go like he was nothing! That's pathetic! No, that's shameful!

A few years earlier Heath retired from the school and on his recommendation I was promoted to the administrator position and how do I repay him? Stabbed in the back! Belittled! Betrayed! That's how. When he left the Club meeting that night he just stopped shooting altogether. We heard now and then about him visiting with to his kids, working his garden, but we steered clear of each other. The Major shook his head, his eyes moistened. Son" he said, visibly shaken by the out pouring of all that emotion, "it was all my fault! My stupid, pig-headed pride that drove him away and for what? What? he slammed his fist onto the arm of the chair. For what?"

"Major is this what has you so down? I interrupted, something that happened what, thirty years ago?"

"I'm not gonna lie to you, I'm sick, real sick but knowing I wronged a good man and not having the chance to make it right before I'm gone, well that's almost to much to bear. Too much…"

His wife made her way across the tiny room and gently wrapped her arms around his neck and they wept over the pain and loss of a dear friend. It was time for me to leave. I grabbed my coat and moved swiftly to the door but stopped just as I reached for the knob and called back,

"Major, my uncle Nick once told me something I'll never forget, he said you haven't failed until you stop trying. I'll see you again, soon. Major. Real soon."

THE ELECTION

—————⟫●⟪—————

Though my attorney friend was finally available this weekend—*sure now her case load is current!*—I just couldn't get the Major off my mind: his state of mind, the desperation in his voice. I had to do something. Sunday, I found my way back to the apartment complex for the third time in as many weeks, but this time I had no intention of seeing the Major. This week I had to find Mr. Heath Roberts.

The directory posted at the entrance gave me the apartment number and the *greeters* who were now comfortable with me hanging around let me in and then helped me to get my bearings. I worked my way around corners down new corridors, past a community room, and finally over to his wing. I can navigate through. I unmarked forests with nothing but a compass and a topo map but struggle through this sprawling ambiguous facility! Funny how the more the designers of these human warehouses try to create little differences in décor, the more it all just looks alike. Reminds me of new age music same sound, different rhythm, the carpet in this hallway was beige and the doors maroon! *Now that's mixing it up!*

Anyway, I worked my way down the beige hallway and found the heavy metal door with the little typed name slipped under the holder—eye level if you're five and half feet tall!: Roberts. I hesitated at the door, gathered my thoughts, and knocked gently. A few seconds past slowly and then I heard some rustling inside and muffled conversation. I'm sure they, whoever they were, were not expecting any visitors today. The door opened and I was face to chest with a very large young man. Obviously not the Mr. Roberts I had expected.

"Can I help you?"

"I…ah…I mean I'm looking for Mr. Heath Roberts." I took a half step backwards in the hallway so I could see this guy's face and not to mention maybe get a step or two ahead if he attacked!

"I'm Colin Roberts. You're asking for my grandfather, this is his apartment. What do you want?"

I introduced myself and explained that I was the foreman down at the club project and just wanted to meet Mr. Roberts whom I had heard about from other members I met over the past several months. Since Colin had the size of an NFL tight-end, I don't think they were all that threatened by me and decided to let me come in. A fact, by the way, not totally lost on my dim wits as I steadied myself for what I had planned. If it all went wrong, getting yelled at might be the least of my worries.

The Mr. Roberts was even more elderly than the Major, which made sense since he was his boss and mentor. He was smaller in stature than the Major, bald except for thinning hair above each ear that most likely will never need cut again. He was dressed in blue slacks, light polo shirt and smart sweater. Dignified and intelligent were my first impression.

"Granddad, Colin said in way of introduction, this man's the foreman down at the development that's going in on the old club ground."

Mr. Roberts listened and let the information connect, then turned to me and smiled cautiously. "So, why are you here? I haven't been involved with the club for years."

"I know sir. It's not really about the property." My eye caught sight of Colin stirring, not that I had ever completely lost sight of him. You couldn't. He was that big! I began to sweat.

"I mean its sorta…that is…well I met someone out there that told me a little bit about the club and all the work you did there, especially in the beginning. He showed me a bunch of old photos, told me how you were the main force in getting the trap leagues going, how you worked with the other clubs to make the industrial league a success. All in all he really credits you with a lot, if not most of the stuff that went on out there so I just wanted to meet you myself."

Mr. Roberts just stared at me. I don't know if I was talking to fast or if it had been that long since anyone spoke to him about the club or he just couldn't grasp the detail of all the stuff I laid on him. Colin stood up and believe me, there was a *lot* of Colin *to* stand up. My throat went dry to balance out the profusion of sweat streaming down both sides of my face.

After a few tense—at least for me—moments that past at roughly the same speed of a melting glacier, Mr. Roberts nodded in acknowledgment. Thoughts come slowly to octogenarians, but they do come. "So, you've met the Major have you?"

"Yes sir, I have." And there it was.

The old man looked down at his soft brown slippers tensing visibly, then out the crystal-clean first floor window at his left. My gaze followed his to the mix of hardwood trees lining the west side of the property where we found the sky leaden, the wind strengthening from the south, and rain imminent. Just about right, I thought to myself expecting a storm of a different kind to rain down on my head at any moment. From the brewing storm outside to his hulking grandson Mr. Roberts turned slowly only to discover that he suddenly found fascination in his own footwear and chose to avoid looking at either of us. Finally, he turned his attention to me, drilling me with an icy stare. He looked me straight in the eye and with lips pursed so tight they were losing color he hissed out his challenge: "Now what?"

I hadn't thought that far. Yeah smart al-lick, now what is right! Now I was the one trying to figure out what to say and what to think. Man, he must've been one heck of a principal. Probably had more than one wayward teen heading home to change his underwear after a scolding!

Colin stood and I braced for an ungraceful exit dangling from his massive arms. He said, "Would you like some coffee?"

"Would I? Oh man would I like some coffee!" I all but yelled, letting out a sigh of relief. After I realized that my immediate safety was not in danger, I turned my attention back to Mr. Robert's question. "The Major" I said beginning my plea, "well sir, he's in the east wing here and…"

"Yeah, what of it? he demanded as he leaned forward staring me down, He's been there for several years. I know that."

"Well, ah yes sir I know you know he's here, but did you know that he was, I mean is very ill? One thing I think that would mean a lot to him, something he'd really like to do is find a way to make things right between the two of you. You know, before it's…well, while he can."

"He said that?"

"Well, yes. As a mater of fact sir, he did." I lied convincingly.

"Do you know what happened out there?" he asked.

He told me about the expansion that he wanted and you didn't and so…"

"Bull! It wasn't about expanding the club and he knows it! It was about the presidency and his taking over the club by forcing me out!"

"I thought he was the president?" I asked taking the coffee offered by Colin.

"Yeah, sure he was the first president but he wasn't the only president of that club. What happened was he was pushing not only to expand the things the members had already agreed to as part of the previous years budget, the ranges and improvements to the old farm house we used as our clubhouse and so forth. No that wasn't enough, once the Major started the changes the cost to do them just kept growing and growing till he showed up one night with blueprints for a whole new clubhouse built just for the trap shooters. First of all, that money was in the general fund, it came from all the members, trap, pond, archery, and black powder, everybody! And second, there just wasn't enough to do it all. Period! But the Major had it figured out; he would take out a second mortgage on the club and use our trees for collateral. Those trees made that club, kept the noise down by providing a buffer between us, and the homes along the road. They kept us safe by giving us a natural backstop for the trap field, the archery course, and rifle ranges. If we lost those trees, we'd lose the club."

Mr. Roberts had to sit back and take a breath. I watched Colin to see if he was going to intercede, but he just sat there with his coffee apparently lost in his own thoughts. Just as well for me I figured. "Mr. Roberts, I didn't come here to open old wounds. I—"

"Well Buddy, you did! You see the Directors were deadlocked on this. We had to come up with a recommendation to the rank and file the following night. I was the president and it was up to me to cast the vote and break the tie. The Major knew how I would vote so he forced a special election at the general meeting, took a lot of arm twisting too to get three-fourths of the members attending to agree to it. I was railroaded, pure and simple."

Mr. Roberts was old and frail but now shaking with anger. "Well sir, I wasn't there that night" I interjected, "but I was at the Major's last week and he'd really like to make things right if you would let him."

It seemed as though he was ignoring both me and the Major's offer, though the later was a pure fabrication by me, for reconciliation. I sipped my coffee slowly and was planning my final argument when Mr. Roberts, still looking down at the floor whispered "How's Edie and the kids?"

"She's fine. Their all fine," I returned respectfully.

"Did he tell you that I'm the kids' godfather?"

"Uh no sir he didn't. I just really met him last fall. I was wrapping things up out at the Club one night, and he came by to bury his hat and we—"

"Bury his hat" Mr. Roberts interrupted.

"Yeah, it was some brown thing all shot up and—"

"He buried his 50-straight hat did he?"

"Well, yeah I guess that's what it was."

"Did he tell you how it got shot up" Mr. Roberts asked with a smirk?

"Yes sir, he did and showed me the photo too."

"Stinkin' Goode...Good old Peaty," Mr. Roberts said more or less to himself and then struggled to get to his feet. Colin stood quickly to help him up as he excused himself and left his massive grandson and me alone in a way to small of a living room. I caught Colin's eye and motioned as if to ask if I should leave? "Naw," he said. "This is the most granddad has spoken in months." Then after a pause, "So you're the foreman down there huh? Any chance you can put a good word in for me? I could use the work."

The request caught me off guard, and I all but dropped my coffee. "Sure, I mean okay, what do you do," I stuttered trying mid-way to remember what a boss was supposed to sound like?

"I just want to get introduced to whoever awards the contracts for subs," he continued. "I have my own grader and backhoe and really need a break. It's tough to come into an area where the same guys have been holding the local work for years. I'm small potatoes compared to most of these guys, but on the other hand all I got is me, so I can pretty much guarantee the crew will show up."

We laughed at that and I said, "Well, Colin, consider yourself introduced to the guy that awards the contracts." He looked a bit sheepish and you know that ain't so easy for a man that size. He just sorta nodded. "So, I continued in my most O-fficial voice, "you insured?"

"Sure am, he replied. See I was trained by the Army Corps of Engineers and was stationed in the Mid-East for a while where I—"

"You've got to be kidding! I was in AK. Must've mustered out about the time you joined up." Our little army reunion was short lived and ended abruptly with Mr. Roberts return, heralded by the unmistakable sound of a porcelain flush echoing from the other side of the bedroom door.

"Young man," Mr. Roberts said without sitting down, signaling to me that it was time for me to leave "tell ya what. I'll sleep on it. Come back next Sunday and we'll see where it goes."

I thanked him and gave Colin my business card on the way out. Regardless of what happens between the

Major and Mr. Roberts I will do what I can to get Colin some work. I've been there. Man have I been there. Just looking into his eyes reminded me of how hard it was for me to get back into civilian work. I can't imagine how much harder it must be to start a new business.

All those thoughts disappeared as soon as the door closed behind me and turning them once again back to the Major. I repeated out loud as I found my way out, hold on Major, just hold on.

BETRAYAL

I really hadn't thought about stopping at the Major's after visiting Mr. Roberts, but I found myself turning up the hallway and into his wing instead of going directly to my truck. Well, I justified to myself, football's over, baseball's exhibition season is weeks away, basketball sorry, is just redundant and if I want to see a good fight I'll go to the Roadhouse on Saturday night not turn on a Hockey game!

Okay, excuses and justification complete. I'm feeling guilty for misleading Mr. Roberts, feeling stupid for getting involved where I probably shouldn't, and feeling confused for not knowing why I couldn't just walk away from these guys. I mean, really, I'd met the Major just last year, how the blazes did I let myself get this close? Questions I'd asked myself before and will probably ask again with the same outcome. Heck if I know!

The Major's wife answered the knock as usual and as she let me slip past we exchanged forced smiles. I thought she looked a bit worn, probably worrying about him, and as I looked past her and saw the sullen form slumped in the rocker recliner I couldn't say I blamed her.

"Hey, you awake in there?" I called quietly.

The Major looked up blankly. "Sure come on in and have a seat. You runnin' a bit behind today or what?"

"No, well, maybe. Just a little." The truth was I hadn't thought about the time and if I had I never woulda figured he'd notice.

"Well, you know how it is Major, when you're not on the clock you kinda just lose track sometimes." I hated to lie to anyone and felt even worse by the end of this exchange. "You look better today." The lies kept pouring out like eating potato chips, once you start...

"Yeah, better than what?" he replied obviously annoyed. Then more to himself then to me he muttered, "no matter, as he slumped back into the chair no matter Atoll!"

"C'mon Major, you gotta snap out of this." I said in a voice that even startled me.

"Really, he said looking up with no expression, says who?"

"We'll, crap. I mean, I know you don't feel good and stuff, but you have all of us worried." So now I was one of the "us" in his life. No longer them and me, now it was "us" and the Major caught it. *This otta be interesting.*

"Oh, I have you *all* worried, do I?"

"Yes you do, and another thing you still haven't finished telling me the rest of the expansion story you started last week either. You can't just leave me hanging like that."

What spark of a smile that seemed to be glowing blew out suddenly, "Sure I have." he said curtly turning back inside himself and staring blankly out the window.

"Well Major, I've been all over the Kauffman farm now and man you really could've done a lot with that property!"

The old man turned slowly towards me and smiled. Well at least the corners of his mouth turned upwards. I think. Now that I had his attention I started my rehearsed confession, "Major, I have something to tell you."

"So, go ahead, what's on your mind, son."The Major searched my eyes for sincerity or honesty or whatever they teach at the university as defense against the lies of students. I felt his authoritative stare even as I found ways to avoid it.

"Well Major, you were right, I did get here a bit later than usual. You see, I had another stop to make before coming over." I began to sweat for the second time today. The Major's wife came in and sat at the tiny diner table just off to my left. I cleared my throat and tried to swallow, which by the way had suddenly filled with baseball sized wads of cotton!

"I, uh, that is earlier today, I met Mr. Roberts."

There it was, served at him like a ninety-five-miles-per-hour curveball. He never saw it coming. I waited, watching his eyes that were avoiding my stare. I worried that it might be too much for the frail old man. I waited some more. The silence was deafening. The small cuckoo clock ticked loudly. I could hear folks outside the apartment in the hallway ushering their Sunday afternoon visitors in and out, the kids running and laughing loudly, having way too much energy to be cooped up inside, and just wanting to get out and run. I knew how they felt. Oh how I wanted to run!

Finally the old man, with considerable effort righted himself leaned forward in my direction causing the chair to squeak as its springs readjusted to his sedentary weight. "Son, he paused, Why? Why would you do that?"

"Well sir, you said he was here in this building. You told me how much you respected Mr. Roberts." I tried to put it back on him. *Self defense I developed a long time ago. Don't ask.* "You've told me all about the guys at the Club, good and bad and well, most of them are gone now. But here was a chance to meet one of your old friends. I just wanted to meet one of the guys in the photo album you keep showing me in person"

"Well?" The Major's voice betrayed his interest and a flood of emotion. His wife stood and moved as if she was going to join her husband and then stepped back and quietly returned to her seat, hands folded, eyes moistening, she pulled a soft handkerchief from the pocket of her apron. She didn't know what to do or say either.

"Well..." I repeated his word to me picking up his last thought. His grandson Colin was there. Boy is he big," I said avoiding going directly to the point, as usual. "Man I bet he coulda been some football player somewhere ..."

"He did play. The Major said flatly. Defensive End at the University, started all four years. Now, what about Heath?"

"Yeah, well, Mr. Roberts, well I wasn't there long but as we talked about the club and stuff, I told him I thought that you might want to get together with him and..."

"What!?" The Major flashed red and sprang his chair upright so fast it scared me.

"Johnny, wait. The Major's wife broke in. What did Heath say, please what did he say?" She always had a calming effect on the Major and as she intervened, perhaps for me, maybe for the Major. She swept over to his chair and placed an arm around his neck.

"He said he'd sleep on it and let me know next Sunday." I intentionally directed my answer to his wife; I could see the Major's jaw tighten violently. His mind trying to grasp the facts and possibilities and perhaps how best to tell me off!

His wife encircled his neck now with both arms, her face pulled to his and I knew he had to feel her tears running down the wrinkles of her cheeks. "Oh, do you really think he'd see us?" She asked with pleading eyes.

My voice surprisingly calm and confident, "Yes ma'am, I do. I watched the Major's eyes dart back to the photo album, over to his kids' pictures on the TV and finally to the knife. Eventually and after another torturous silence his eyes pierced mine. I met his stare and then braced for the inevitable question; "What the Sam-hill did you talk about over there?"

I hesitated, I really didn't want to go there but I had used up my quota of lies for the day. "The election," I said as gently as I knew how.

"Oh my. Oh my." The Major and his wife both said first under their breath and then to each other. After another tense pause, the Major straightened in his chair, pulled his shoulders back and braced himself. "Anything else?"

"Yes sir, he asked about your wife and kids."

"Son of a..."

"Johnny, don't. Just don't!" His wife interrupted the outburst and retreated to the safety of the bedroom, the slamming door punctuating the pain she felt at their loss.

We both sat there looking at the door long after his wife disappeared. Then, still looking at the closed door I said, "Major I hope I haven't..."

"Son, take a breath would you please or at least, for crying out loud, let me take one! Do you have any idea how long it's been since Heath has spoken to Edie or I? You gotta try to get this through your head, when all this happened Heath already had several grandkids. Shoot, they'd babysit for us almost every week. Colin was still in diapers. Heath would bring him over and he'd crawl all over my two. Tom would take him outback and roll balls to him. They had a great time. Heath had just retired and pushed me into his position at the school. We were always in their home or they or their kids were in ours. I'm telling you we couldn't have been closer if we were blood-kin! Are you starting to get this yet? Heath Roberts was my mentor, my friend, and godfather to my kids. I would have fought for him or his kids any day, any place no questions asked. Do you know what that kind of friendship is like?"

"No sir. Honestly I don't. I've always been a loner, you know, odd man out as it were."

"That's really too bad, you have no idea what you've missed," He said sincerely.

"I didn't sir, but I'm starting to get the picture."

"So he told you about the election. What did he say exactly?"

Flank attack! Ha! No way I'm getting pulled into this old fight. I was trying to get them to forget the thing so I wasn't about to throw gasoline onto that old fire! I suddenly found that I hadn't really used up all my lies after all and got creative with the truth.

"Not much." I mumbled. I felt the Major's glare. "Really Major it was a short visit. All he said was that you wanted the expansion to move faster than he thought it should, and you beat him in an election to get it past."

"Humph! That might be the way he saw it," He growled "Crap, maybe that was what happened. Maybe I was just too darned smart for my own good? Maybe…"

"You see that year," he continued, "the election was really close. By then the club was so big we had little clubs within the club all wanting to do stuff of their own. Archery, black powder, Trap, Small bore rifle, pistol guys, man were we growing fast! The by-laws stipulated that an incumbent president had to have at least three-fourth of a voting quorum to get elected for a second term and had to take at least two years off after that. We figured if a guy was really bad there was no way he'd get three-fourth's vote."

"Well Heath wasn't bad, wasn't bad at all, but we disagreed and I was being egged-on by some of the leaders of the little clubs that wanted to have more stuff, and Heath was always telling them they had to wait till we had the cash in hand. We knew that if elected, this would be Heath's last term regardless and with some of the more vocal guys behind me, I started campaigning and making all kinds of promises, some of them real whoppers too! But what tore us apart is when I got Goode to back me. He had a small group of elitist friends—no that's too kind, they were out and out snobs, but I needed the votes. I got the votes and got the presidency back. Heath walked out when the votes were counted and never came back. The club moved forward and I lost a dear friend which I've regretted every day since."

The Major slumped back showing serious fatigue, and I knew I had to end the visit soon, but hesitated trying to let the images and emotion sink in. How in the world can a small group of friends set out to buy a piece a property to do some after-work shooting and messing around with dogs and whatnot turn into a life altering knockdown drag out fight? I think the Major must have read my thoughts.

"I know, and you're right. Seems stupid to me now, but you shoulda been there. Man it was intoxicating."

"Whatever you say Major. Guess I'll just have to take your word for it sir." I let slip not meaning to be judgmental but sounding that way none the less. It struck me that for the first time since we met, I was confronted with the man's imperfection, in a conciliatory tone he asked quietly, "When did you say you were going back to see Heath?"

"Next Sunday," I advised as I stood to leave.

The Major slumped back into his chair, "Another week then, is it?"

"Yes he wants time to sleep on it."

"He always did."

"Major," I called back quietly as I reached the door.

"Yeah?"

"Major, I think you should too."

The Major's eyes moistened and with a nod that I returned, acknowledging his gratitude I hesitated long enough to see him reach for the photo album that would transport him back to more gentle times when the Club was a place where two friends could meet, shoot, and share something no else could understand. Men of like passion.

END AROUND

——➤●◄——

About mid-week I called Colin and let him know I was having a bidders meeting for interested subs and invited him to join. He answered the call on the first ring—guess things really were slow—and seemed genuinely grateful for the opportunity. Heck, I know what it's like to muster out and try to start over in civilian life. One day you have everyone above the rank of Spec-5 telling you when to eat, sleep, work, and what to think and the next you are on your own. Some money in your pockets a worn duffle on your shoulder and no one watching your back! He deserved a shot and I meant to see he got one regardless of how things turned out with Mr. Roberts.

The meeting was predictably uneventful with my simple agenda: *get your coffee and donut, sit down, listen up, here's the work, how to quote it and if you get the job, here's how you get paid.* Nothing fancy about me or what I do, but I think these no-nonsense, hard-nosed guys appreciated it. If they wanted grip-and-grin crap, they'd all be wearing suits drinking cappuccinos and talking about their golf scores and hedge funds. These guys live in khakis and work boots; they drive their three-quarter ton, crew-cab pick-ups everywhere with names on the doors like J.B Prince and Son General Contracting, Bold River Excavating, and Thomas and Stonne Masonry.

187

Then there was Colin. A one man show and obviously the small fish in the retention pond but he did okay. He made himself known, handed out a bunch of fresh business cards, and it looked as though he may have made some real solid leads. Even if I couldn't hire him straight up, I hoped he got some work through the general contractors. These gen-cons have a great business model, they lined up the work, hired independent guys like Colin, paid them on a cost-plus basis, and pocketed the profit without investing in equipment or labor. Worked out for everyone.

"Colin, I called over as the meeting was wrapping up, can I see ya for a second?"

"Sure," he said breaking away from his spot at the door shaking hands with everyone as they left. He was really working the room. I think some of the guys recognized him from his playing days. "So, what's up?"

"Well two things, first I want you to know that I'm going to give you a fair shot at any work you bid on regardless of how things turn out with the Major. Complete the sub-contractor information sheet with references and attach a copy of your COI, and I'll deliver it to our attorney."

I thought he was a little taken aback and maybe a bit weary of the generosity. Quid-pro-Quo is all too common in this line of work. "Well, thanks, I appreciate it." He said kicking around the carpet with a boot that had to be a size fifteen! "So, what else is on your mind?"

"Your grandfather. I visited the Major after I left his place last week and he's not good. We, I mean they really don't have a handle on it but just looking at him and you know it's bad."

"So what do you have in mind?"

"I just want to be sure, well these are two pretty old guys that haven't seen each other for a long while and well, crap Colin I'm just not sure how they will take seeing each other after all that went down between them. You know?"

"Yeah, I thought about that too. Grandpa didn't say much after you left Sunday, he just sat there looking out the window. He'd sort'a smile then bite his lip or clinch his bony fist. I could see it all working on him hard. But you know what?"

"No, what?" I replied fearing Colin was about to call it all off.

"I think we…"

We! Cool he's on my side!

"…outta work it out, but slowly."

"I'm listening."

"I was thinking about it and decided to call my dad. He is about ten years older than Tom, the Major's son and remembers the Major back in the day. Well Dad agrees and wants to help bring them back together and has an idea on how to approach it. Let's call it an End-Around."

"Okay, what d'ya want me to do?"

"First talk to the Major and get him to meet with my dad and me. Make it this Sunday if possible. Then we'll try to get Grandpa to agree to meet the Major and assuming it's a go, which it will be—"

"You sure?" I interrupted. Mr. Roberts made quite an impression on me, and I wasn't all that confident myself.

"Yeah, I'm sure. Trust me on this one. He may make you sweat a little, but he wants to see the Major just as much as the Major wants to see him. But pride being what it is we have to make sure they can both arrive and leave, holding their heads high. You know?"

"Makes sense."

"Okay, you come in and do the dance with Grandpa, and then when you go to leave dad and I will *walk you out*. We'll tell Grandpa before you get there that we want to talk over some work thing or other so he won't be suspicious. When we leave Grandpa's place, the three of us run over to the Major's."

"All good, just one thing."

"Yeah, what's that?"

"I gotta call Tom...just in case."

"Yeah," he said rubbing the back of his head. "that's probably a good idea at that."

We left that day still pondering the what-ifs and scheduled a meeting Friday so I could get Colin's sub-apps, and go over the final plan for Sunday. The next day I called Tom to talk him through the scenario. He wasn't thrilled at the prospect of the two old friends-turned-adversaries getting together.

"Wow, I dunno if that's a good idea, man, wow," He stammered.

"Uh Tom, I sorta already told your dad I met Mr. Roberts. I mean go ahead and call him man if that would help but I am sure your dad really wants to make this right. Down deep I think, no man, I *know* Mr. Roberts does as well."

"Let me talk to Sis. She should know about this too. Just wait till I call you back, okay?"

"Okay, but I am meeting again with Colin Friday and..."

"You mean Colin the one that played Defensive End at the University?" he interrupted.

"Yeah, why?

"Well it's just I didn't know he was back. I'd heard he'd enlisted after he blew out his knee and his girlfriend dropped him. Heard he took it all pretty hard too. Just surprised he came back to Delphia that's all."

"I really don't know about any of that Tom. Colin and I only spoke about work and getting your dad and Mr. Roberts back together.

"Well, I'll call Sis and get back to you."

I holstered the blackberry and let out a groan. How the heck did I get in the middle of this? The image of the final scene in *The Sand Pipers* ran through my head. The other sailors had just pulled Cybil Sheppard to safety and left Steve McQueen to hold off the Boxer's closing in for the kill. Wounded with no where to go he sat down and yelled 'I was almost home! What happened? I was almost home!' And with that there was a final le-cu-de-crass shot and he slumped. A man caught up in someone else's fight and not knowing how he got there. Boy could I relate!

How did I go from loner-drifter foreman fresh from the Army to getting mixed up in not one but two families? People I didn't even know existed a year ago. What happened? I met a man at a trap club, just an old man at an old defunct gun club. I wondered how many other men have had similar changes in direction by meeting someone special. How did the Major phrase that again, "men of like passion."

Well I've gone this far and now with a pending job offer that will take me far from Delphia, the club and the Major sitting on my desk, a job too good to ignore, I want to see this through. I have to see this through.

CONSPIRATORS

———————

S aturday blew by even with a quiet date with a certain brilliant brunette attorney sandwiched between my Friday meeting with Colin and my tense phone call to Tom. Sunday was on me before I knew it. Normally, I'd be in the sack till mid-morning but not today. I was up and e-mail open ready to send a response accepting an invitation to interview for a job down south. Seems the economy is closing a lot of golf courses that are being turned into lower cost housing. The job would put me in charge of a team of on-site foremans who would direct a bevy of sub-contractors. It would be my responsibility to represent a bunch of cutthroat bankers—um I mean venture capitalists by negotiating contracts with suppliers of material and coordinate the use to control waste. Efficient and cheap means assembly line housing developments with mirror image floor plans, intersecting yards, and small garages at the end of drives just long enough to pull a decent size SUV off the street. Whatever, I just have to get them built; I don't have to live there! I had developed a good reputation at the club job, operating under budget with very few issues from the subs and no visits to court. I don't have an MBA, but it's not that difficult. Sorta doing what we learned in the army, define the requirements, measure the performance, address issues quickly and decisively. Too many managers let poor performance fester. Address it head on with no emotion and move on. We're building houses for crying out loud not performing surgery! Anyway the offer was just too good to pass up, but I would be leaving Delphia and probably my attorney friend behind forever…one thing at a time.

I clicked the mouse and off my e-mail flew at the speed of light. I wondered if the Major ever had a PC? Of course not! He's from the typewriter and mimeograph days. Blue smelly rollers copying test after test for his classes. I can just see him standing in a sun-drenched room surrounded by all that chemical smell dreaming about his glorious Club. I bet he ran out of paper more then once thinking about the last target missed or some odd catastrophe or other more then once. My idle thoughts about the Major, mimeograph's and e-mail were interrupted by the vibrating Blackberry. It was Tom.

"Hello Tom" I answered flatly, "what's the verdict?"

"Well Sis and I talked, talked a lot actually, and we won't interfere with your plan but…"

Always a 'but' I thought to myself. "Yes, but what?"

"But" he said with emphasis, "Sis and I want to be there too."

"Sure, no problem, except I'm not exactly sure *where* is and when *there* will be as yet." I said honestly. So I told him Colin's plan again so there was no misunderstanding, I would visit Mr. Roberts today and get his okay, then Colin and his Dad would go with me to the Major's to break the ice.

"Sounds reasonable" Tom whispered, I think to himself. Sounds like it might work. One more thing," "Yeah, what's that?" I asked, starting to get a bit antsy. "Call me this afternoon and let me know how it turns out."

"You got it." I promised.

I drove slowly to the retirement home, having left way too early for my one o'clock visit. As I turned the radio down and watched the landmarks pass one at a time, I couldn't help but think back on my first visit, the suspicious retirees sitting at the entrance, the Major all bundled up sitting out back by the fountain, the beat-up thermos filled with coffee and the stories, oh how I enjoyed the stories. To this day, I still only got half of them, but I know something else too. I'm a better man having spent time with the Major. What a year!

I pulled into a parking spot as far away from the Major's wing as possible and made my way to Mr. Robert's place. If things didn't go well, I planned a fast escape. Colin answered the door, and I searched his face for a hint as to what Mr. Robert's answer was going to be but got nothing beyond common courtesy. Colin ushered me in and introduced me to his dad. A pleasant quiet man, I'd guess mid sixties and wherever Colin got his size, it sure wasn't from him! He was about my height, thinning gray hair which gave him the appearance of a retired educator or minister. Maybe what they said about all the steroids in our meat causing this generation to outgrow their parents was true!

195

"Have a seat," Mr. Roberts commanded and pointed me towards a hard-straight, backed kitchen chair placed in the living room I'm sure just for me. "You have a good week?" He asked unexpectedly.

"Uh, yeah, sure it was okay" I replied obviously uneasy and out numbered. I looked to Colin for support but found he was currently enthralled with the beige carpet under his massive boots. "I mean, yeah we had a good week" I repeated as the realization of having to go this alone swept over me.

"Colin told us about going to the bidders meeting. Got some good leads too. Looks like he has some work booked as soon as the ground dries out a bit"

"I hope it works out," I said honestly and with that there was a long pause interrupted only by the clearing of throats and a nervous cough or two. I couldn't take it any longer. "Sir, I've spoken with Tom and he called his sister, and they'd like to be there, you know if you agree of course, when you and the Major get together." Colin decided it was a good time to make coffee. Not a good sign for the effort I feared.

"Well about that, Mr. Roberts started cautiously, I'm still not sure it's a good idea. It's been an awfully long time, and there were a lot of hard feelings." Mr. Roberts was hedging. I had to push a little, maybe he just wanted to reassured that the Major was sincere?

"Sir," I began what I knew would be my final plea, "I'm not sure when you last saw the Major, but he isn't the man he once was, shoot he isn't even the man he was a year ago when I met him. I think all these memories he shared with me, the auction and his failing health are working on him, and not for the good. Sir, I'm asking for you to let him make it right or at least know that he tried. I caught Mr. Roberts eye. Sir, there may not be much time left."

Colin came in with coffee served in unmatched mugs. I noticed that he served his grandfather last and he seemed to make sure he brought it to him turned a certain way. It took Mr. Roberts a few seconds to realize what he had, then he passed a glance at his son and shook his head in submission. The ceramic mug held a faded graphic that turned out to be the club's emblem, crossed long gun, and fishing rod with the words *Delphia Fish and Game Association* written below.

Looking at his son and grandson, Mr. Roberts finally and for the first time since I met him let a smile creep onto his face, "You guys. Mother would be so proud. Oh how she loved to put it over on me, didn't she? Okay," he said losing the smile and turning back to me, "okay, if the Major wants to meet, we'll meet. How about the community room in this wing?"

"Great idea sir! Thank you!"

"Don't thank me yet, we still don't know how this is all going to turn out now do we? I might just freeze up and walk out."

"Somehow sir, I doubt that very much."

As planned I excused myself and Colin and his dad said they'd walk me out. Mr. Roberts just looked at them accusingly and said, "Yeah, right, okay, I'll just wait here with this beat up coffee mug." Knowing we were busted, we left as fast as we could get three men through that tiny kitchen door.

As I led our party to the Major's, we walked without conversation, each lost in our own thoughts. What my co-conspirators were thinking I couldn't have guessed, my thoughts were all over the map, Mr. Roberts, The Major, Colin, my attorney friend, my trip this week to interview...The Major.

RECONCILIATION

W e three, that is, my two conspirators, Colin, his dad and I left Mr. Roberts under the guise of *them* walking *me out* whatever that was supposed to mean, it opened the door for phase two of our plan to reunite Mr. Roberts and the Major. We hurried from Mr. Roberts's wing down the connecting hallways distinct only in variations of earth-toned carpet and walls. We slowed just short of the Major's door to catch our breath and pass a silent glance between ourselves after which I stepped ahead to knock softly on the door, a sound I'm sure the Major and his wife recognized and maybe even looked forward to each week.

I heard the steps inside coming to answer the door but there was a longer then usual delay on having it open. I suspected the Major's wife looked through the little peephole and had to collect herself a bit before inviting us in, trying to imagine what effect it would have on the failing health of her husband. The door open tentatively, I watched the small elderly woman for signs of resistance, but her eyes went quickly past me and right to Colin's dad.

"Hi Johnny," she whispered as she wrapped her arms around his neck and then it hit me, he was named after the Major, and I wasn't even close to grasping the depth of this friendship!

"Hello Aunt Edie, he said with a warm smile and embrace with familiar affection as if there was never a separation between the families. And this is Colin," he said simply as he released her and stepped aside to present his son.

"I've heard so much about you Colin, please come in, the Major is in the living room."

She heard about Colin? Really, from exactly who I wondered for crying out loud? My thoughts were racing, questioning myself, trying to decide if I was being played by either side or both! No place to hide now, I'll just ride it out and try to escape with my skin intact.

We found the Major in his chair and for the first time in many weeks, actually dressed and an extra chair already in place. I wondered if he knew we were coming, how? Tom!

"Hi John, he said some what formally I thought, this must be Colin. The young man bent over and shook the elder's hand warmly. Have a seat, the Major offered and then took command. How's your dad, John?" There it was, right there in front of us. The Major knew what he was doing and so did we. We just had to walk down the path he was leading us.

"He's okay Uncle John," he answered on queue. "We've been talking about us getting together for lunch sometime soon." *Great lead Johnny Ol' boy, keep it going man!* I cheered silently.

The Major's wife came in and sat on the arm of his chair, much to his annoyance. "Edie, please, he said straining to look around her. You guys want some coffee or anything?"

"Sure, sounds good," we all said for the Major's benefit. Guy thing. Always the accommodating hostess as she dutifully, if not enthusiastically left for the kitchen.

"So the Major continued, your Dad is up for," he hesitated, "uhm lunch?

Okay I thought this will work. Our mission now had a code name, Operation Lunch!

Playing along perfectly Colin said "Maybe we can call Tom and Sis to see if they want to come over too? I'm sure Granddad would like to see them."

"Yeah," I said "it'd be quite a reunion..." *Silence! Crap, I did it again. Crap!*

"Yes, the Major finally whispered, a reunion, a family reunion."

"How's next Sunday?" Colin's Dad asked sensing it was time to close the deal.

"Edie?" The Major called toward the kitchen.

"That would be fine, she replied as lightly as she could, just fine."

"Fine," Colin said nodding to his dad who just smiled.

Very fine I thought to myself. Very fine *and fi-nal-ly!* Having agreed to coffee we had to finish at least a cup a piece as well as a round of her freshly baked cookies which lead to some inside joke between the elders leaving Colin and I scratching our heads a bit. That's okay I thought, we didn't just break the ice today, we freaking shattered it!

With some more hugs and warm smiles, a few tears and a couple pats on the back we made our way out of the Major's apartment. We split up at the intersection of the two wings; I headed out for my truck leaving Colin and his dad to discuss details of the "Lunch" with Mr. Roberts. Truth was, I already thought about how I could convince my attorney friend to meet me somewhere half-way between our two towns for dinner and some...conversation.

The week was hectic, even though my current boss knew about the pending interview I still had a lot of loose ends to wrap up with bids, suppliers, and laborers. With all that going on, I managed to fly down, nail the interview and return home knowing I had the job if I wanted it and all the while thinking about the Major and his reunion with Mr. Roberts.

Colin and Tom who took the lead in securing the room and arranging the catering, were passing e-mails hot and heavy, *cc*'ing me and Colin's dad to keep us in the loop. The day had been set last week and agreed to by Mr. Roberts. Colin said his granddad just kinda set his jaw then shook his head and said, "So here we go then," and hasn't said much of anything since.

I can only imagine the emotion stored up in these men who have had little outside of family to think back on as they days pass slowly sitting there looking out their windows. What do they remember? The shooting for sure, the work, the in-fighting over what now has to seem stupid to both of them. How do men let there pride drive them away from what they really love? I hoped it wasn't my pride driving me south and away from what might be here. Time will tell. Same thing with the Major and Mr. Roberts, only time will tell.

———

I arrived at the retirement home early and found some very nervous people milling about the entrance, Colin and his dad, Tom, his sister and mother. They told me the collective families were all waiting in the community room. Colin called his brother who brought his kids; Tom's two were there as well as his sister's husband and their five kids. The adults knew what was afoot of course, and I figured the family's thought there might be safety in numbers if things didn't go as planned so they loaded up the SUVs and made the trek.

"What's up? I asked the committee of LWF—Long Worried Faces—at the door.

"Well, Colin said kicking around the carpet with those big size fifteens, We didn't know who should arrive first."

"You're kidding! I blurted out, but the look on the LWF's said otherwise. People, this isn't the peace talks for crying out loud!"

"No, its not," Tom said seriously, this has way more at stake then mere world peace!"

That's what they needed. It was if the whole group let out a collective sigh of relief, now, to get things moving. "Okay, let's just take a breath and think this out," I said.

"Tom, why don't you go get your dad? Colin, can you go and pick up your granddad? We'll set the Major at a table with John and his wife, and when Colin gets there with Mr. Roberts, um Tom, why don't you greet him at the door with your wife and maybe your mom, if that's okay with you ma'am?" The Major's wife nodded and we all looked at one another one last time before splitting up. As they started to drift away I added, to no one in particular, "after that, well, these guys are going to just have to figure it out on their own."

Then it occurred to me that I had been encircled like a quarterback would've been calling out a play and had to fight back the urge to bring them all back one last time and put their hands in the pile for a go-team yell, but that woulda been over the top... cool, but definitely over the top!

We had a plan everyone seemed to think was at least reasonable. Colin gave Tom a head start so he could be sure the Major would arrive first. Colin and the rest of the team left shortly thereafter leaving me in the foyer alone. Just before I started down the corridor, a painfully bent-over elderly man, dressed in faded green work pants, and khaki shirt struggled past using a walker. He looked up at me and said "You're a good man. We all know what you are doing here. God bless you son." Leaning hard on the walker, he continued his way down the hallway. I think that was the first God-bless-you greeting I ever got that didn't originate with a sneeze! Felt pretty good too, but there was no time to get all teary-eyed and mushy yet!

I hurried down to the community room and found it to be just what you'd expect, high ceiling, large fans that rotated either so fast the paper napkins blew off the table or so slow, they were useless. Alternating green and white twelve inch square tile flooring—*it's the contractor in me*—and big kitchen with counter for serving from inside. There was a large flat-screened TV, mercifully turned off with the remote safely out of reach, folding chairs, and tables throughout with a few sofas, and soft chairs near the bookcases. A good place to escape when those little apartments began to grow a little too small for comfort or host visits from friends and family. *I sure hope that is what happens today!*

The Major arrived as planned, was greeted at the door by John and his wife who led him over to one of the soft chairs. Tom placed a pillow brought with them from the apartment behind the Major's back. The Major's daughter and son-in-law came over got into some small talk about the kids with John leaving the Major somewhat disengaged.

I was trying to stay as inconspicuous as possible, hiding by the punch bowl. The Major glanced my way, and with a knowing look he seemed to have been born with, passed me a nod and a smile. I smiled back and gave him a little thumbs-up which made him laugh a little. Good start I thought to myself.

It seemed like the Major no sooner got settled then the door opened and in came Mr. Roberts leaning on his grandson's arm. Tom stepped up and greeted them warmly. Mr. Roberts was obviously touched and recognized the gesture for just what it was, purely reconciliatory. Tom stepped aside and Mr. Roberts walked directly to the Major who was by now standing, as best he could on his own waiting for his friend to approach.

"Hello Johnny," Mr. Roberts whispered as he held out his hand.

The Major opened his mouth but nothing came out. He looked up trying to get control of his emotions, *C'mon Major* I yelled inside myself, *c'mon for crying out loud!*

"Johnny," Mr. Roberts began again.

The Major looked his friend in the eye, his chest heaving against years of regret and guilt. Finally and just barely audible he answered, "yes sir?"

"It's okay Johnny and thanks for coming to my lunch today."

The Major's shoulders slumped they clasped hands and then arms. Oh the touch of someone you admire and whose company you miss so much, you ache!

"Heath," the Major finally whispered, tears streaming down both sides of his face unashamedly, "Heath I am so sorry, I am so…so…sorry"

"Johnny, I know what you are. You are my friend!"

THE GIFT

⟹⟩●⟨⟸

The lunch didn't go on long. These two old friends had quite a private chat over in a corner while the grandkids played, and the adults made small talk, all the while keeping a watch on the old folks with one eye. After a while the Major's wife wondered over to my table and sat down beside me. We watched the old friends get reacquainted with one another with a lot of head shaking and nodding. Whatever had been lost, the art of communication between these two men who once worked together closely surely wasn't. Neither needed many words to say what they meant.

Mr. Roberts was the first to stand. He said goodbye to the grandkids and I learned later, great-grandkids, and let Colin help him back to his apartment. Before leaving he found me in spite of the confusion and thanked me for my part in getting the "lunch" scheduled.

The Major and his wife followed, and they too thanked me for helping to reintroduce the Major to his old friend. I told them I had some news to share, but it would wait a few weeks. I told them I'd be in touch and snuck out quickly leaving John, Tom, and the combined families laughing, telling stories on each other, and making plans for the next get together. I'm sure they were all relieved about how well the "lunch" came off and avoiding any 911 calls! Can't say I wasn't relieved as well, but for now I just wanted to be alone to start thinking about my move and let the reality of the fact that my next visit to the Major's will most likely be my last.

———•••———

As expected the job offer came quickly and without much fanfare, basically it translated to "if you want it it's yours but you have to let us know now and be here to start on the first of the Month." I submitted my resignation and began to tie up loose ends when I got an e-mail from Tom asking if I could meet him and the Major at the Delphia Tavern?

"Sure, I texted back, but why not at the Major's?"

"No, Tom returned, that wouldn't work."

"Okay," I replied quickly and then entered the date and time in my appointment scheduler. With so many other things going on, I really didn't think too much about it.

When I arrived at the tavern the hostess said that Tom and the Major were in the banquet room reserved for meetings. I found my way back and found in addition to Tom and the Major, Colin, his dad, and Tom's sister.

"What's all this about?" I asked while my mind tried to catch up with what was happening in front of me.

"Well son, the Major started, rumor has it you're moving away."

I glanced a Colin knowing full well he was the only one that could've known through the general contractor he was subbing for over at the Kauffman Farm site.

Colin was kicking around again with those big-boots of his, ignoring my glare.

"Yes sir, I mumbled turning towards the Major. I've taken a job down south."

"Humph, he said turning away from me and toward the group, the way I hears it, you've gone uptown on us, re-formed from ripping up gun clubs to con-verten' old golf courses into civilized housing de-velopments!"

"Yup, guess that about sizes it up sir," I said and everyone had a good laugh at my expense.

"Tom, the Major said getting his son's attention. Let's do this."

"Well, right, okay" Tom began as everyone but he and I took a seat.

Dad and... he gestured around the room, ...really all of us, appreciate you taking the time to visit with him this past year, breaking the ice with Mr. Roberts and bringing the two families back together again and all. And we..."

"Tom!" The Major interrupted.

"Okay, Dad and Sis thought, well you might like to have something to take with you when you move away."

I wasn't prepared for this. Even though the Major has grown to mean a lot to me and I will never forget him. The feisty old man that tried to straighten me out on hunting ethics, educate me in the way of trap shooting and taught more about friendship and loyalty than anyone I ever knew. I could never forget him whether I had anything more tangible then the memories of our fountain meetings or not. And to think it started out as idle curiosity and a lonely young guy trying to fill time on Sunday afternoons!

"Sis…" Tom stepped back and his sister stood up and took the floor.

"When Mom and Dad moved to the apartment, Dad had to give up a lot of his things. For the most part there just wasn't enough room and some things, well he wasn't permitted to take along." As she spoke, I noticed for the first time that she has her mother's soft brown eyes.

On cue, Colin reached under the table where he was seated and gently pulled an aged leather case from beneath his feet, reverently setting it on the table before me.

"Well, the Major broke in taking charge of the presentation one of the things I wasn't permitted to take into the apartment was this old shotgun. It should look familiar to you, since it's in almost all of those old photo's you've been looking at in my album back home."

I placed my hands gently on the case and placed a thumb over each latch. I moved the mechanism's simultaneously snapping them open in unison. A sound the Major seemed to enjoy immensely. Lifting the lid exposed a fine single-barrel trap shotgun, obviously not standard grade. The stock showed some wear on the fore-end and grip, but there were no stains at the receiver from over-oiling, the steel of the barrels was in great shape and was fitted with a slightly higher-then-field rib and two white beads, one in the middle and one at the very end of the barrel. There was a thin rubber butt-pad that probably was added at the Major's request—all in all a beautiful piece.

Perched carefully on the receiver was an old picture of the Major and Mr. Roberts each balancing a shotgun on their shoulders with a small trophy sitting in front of them on a table. The reality of what was transposing in front of me began to settle in.

"Major, I couldn't. I mean how can I..."

"Son, no one here is shooting much trap anymore, and I would sure appreciate it if you'd take care of this old friend for me."

"Take care of it?" I searched his face for more.

He continued in a tone and manner I hadn't heard before, "There are some thing's in life that can't be bought, sold, or even given away. Things like a deer stand, a knife and a fine firearm used and treasured over the years by someone special. These things are always theirs, even... he hesitated, even son after that person passes on.

So you see in our eyes this will always be my gun, the Major's gun until such time when it's time for you to pass it along to the next person to take care of it. Maybe you'll have a son someday, or you'll befriend some whippersnapper asking dumb questions about a shot-up hat!"

We shared a smile over the memory of that first meeting. Sitting in the shade of that old tree and sharing an iced tea. Who'd thought we'd end up here? Surely not me!

"You see son by passing this along, you keep the memory of a man alive. I know men who have been taking care of other men's memories for generations: Merv's shed, Sam's Winchester, Harry Sr.'s Martin Fly Reel, and yes Curt's knife. Some of these men would have been completely forgotten by now if it weren't for the caring for and handing down of these things. That's why it's important to me to commend it to your care. One more thing, this ain't no museum piece. You get settled, wherever the heck you're going and find a trap field, giver a try."

I repeated back to the Major, "Merv's shed, Sam's Winchester, Harry Sr.'s Martin and…" As I gently closed the cover to his case, "the Major's Browning BT99."

"You've got it son," he said as he offered me his hand.

"Major, this means more to me than you'll ever know, but shouldn't it go to a trap shooter?"

"Maybe it has and you just don't know it yet?" he said wryly. We all laughed and the hostess brought us dinner. We picked at our meals and then sat around with coffee visiting like family discussing everything from his daughter's farm, the weather to the cost of contractors and the futility of golf! Long before I was ready for the evening to end, the Major announced he was a bit tired and asked Tom to take him home.

As he stood to leave he put a hand to my shoulder and fighting back genuine emotion he began his farewell:

"Thank you. Meeting you, talking out and sharing all those pent up memories helped to close the book on my life at the club, helped me let loose of a lot of old friends and find the one that I'd thought I had lost forever. Now, keep in touch, will you son?"

I assured him I would. "Major, I said just as he made it to the exit of the little room leaning heavily on Tom, tired and worn down, Someday you just might get the chance to see me shoot your old Browning."

"That would be fine, just fine."

And with that the Major turned and walked out with the others quietly following behind. Colin was the last to leave. He stopped and offered his hand, "I just want you to know I appreciate you getting me work."

"Colin, all I did was get you in the game man, you carried the ball."

He just smiled, turned and walked away.

That left me, the bus staff and the Major's Browning.

All of a sudden I felt very alone.

THE BEGINNING, A FAREWELL

⟫●⟪

It had been a few months since, I left Delphia, mercifully my schedule was tight. I had to get my Foremen in line and acclimated with my way of doing things and keeping an eye peeled for Quid-pro-quo crap. What a world! I hardly had time to think about the Major, my attorney friend, or the club. The Major's shotgun was tucked safely under my bed, a place I fell into every night around 2300 or so after putting in a long fourteen-to-eighteen-hour day, driving hundreds of miles and working through every problem imaginable from disgruntled neighbors to threats by the various unions against my sub-contractors. Finally one rare Sunday off, I found time to call the Major, Tom answered the phone and speaking very quietly said his Dad was not good at all, and in fact he was not expected to last more than a few days. I was stunned.

"T-Tom," I stuttered, "is there anything I can do?"

"No, there is nothing anyone can do, Tom said gently. Dad told me months ago that the doctors had pretty much covered all the possibilities of treatment they could with this type of cancer and that it was just a matter of pain-management from then on."

"You mean he knew all along while we were trying to work things out with Mr. Roberts that his days were actually numbered? And you did to?"

"That is why I was so hesitant, he said, I just wasn't sure the shock wouldn't have made him even worse. Look…" Tom said bringing the call to an abrupt end, "I'll call you when… His voice trailed off, you know, I'll call you when we know more."

I still had the Blackberry at my ear even after the phone went silent. I just stood there with a million images flashing through my mind, the first day we met at the Club, hot and dusty that old blue coupe coming into my equipment staging area, sitting with him in the shade while his wife napped in the car, all the Sundays sitting out back by the fountain, the battered thermos and the ever present coffee. And oh the stories about starting the club, his friends the hunting and the day we traveled out to that big Trap Club where he got to shoot a few targets. What a day that was! Of all the time we shared that may have been my favorite. The Major was genuinely happy when surrounded by men that he knew, maybe not by name, but by what he'd call their passion. Their passion for shooting, competing, trading guns, and ribbing each other about their scores, that was the Major at his best.

Wow, Tom's voice had still echoed in my head, the Major was not expected to… he might be gone soon. My mind raced, how could I get there, in time, to see him? I just got this job started, I have no back up and was told not to even think about getting sick until winter freeze, which down here comes late and is gone early. I had to go, but I couldn't go. I began to pace. I pulled the Major's gun out from under the bed and gently wiped the thin layer of dust from its lid. I open it for the first time since coming here. I don't know why I just did but there it was, the picture I had forgotten about. That picture of the Major and Mr. Roberts holding the shotguns standing in front of the little trophy. I couldn't read the inscription, not that it mattered but I began to draw a mental image of the day, it was hot, the trees were full bloom, and the stern-faced little smiles trying to unsuccessfully disguise the pride of a champion.

I was staring at the picture, burning the memory into my brain. What about Mr. Roberts, his son John, Colin, the Major's wife Edie, and Mildred his old friend's widow? Too many what-ifs that didn't concern me any longer, or did they?

My mind continued to race. I checked the weather. Rain! Lots and lots of rain for the next several days, You gotta love this semi-tropic weather! I called my boss to be sure we were cool, then I called the foremen to be sure they knew what I expected and reminded them what my Blackberry was for, then I threw some clothes in the duffle, gassed the truck, and headed north! Almost seemed like going home.

I pulled into Delphia early Monday morning after eighteen hours of driving on stale quickie-mart coffee and greasy burgers and pulled into the first hotel I came across to grab a room and shower. You'd thought I had been on the road three days as good as that shower felt. Must be getting old! Anyway it was still early so I figured a quick nap was in order before calling Tom and catching up on the Major's condition. No hotel bed ever felt so good...

I was shaken awake when the cleaning staff came in and was just as shaken to find a half-naked body—mine—in the bed they planned to strip and remake. It was eleven o'clock! I told them to skip me today, splashed some water on my face, dressed quickly as I could, ran down the two flights of steps and fired the one-ton diesel up. I didn't know you could throw stones with a dually, but I did that day!

I made my way to the retirement home where some of the regulars sitting at the entrance remembered me as the Major's young friend and told me what hospital he was in. I knew exactly where it was and sped that direction with a weird sense of urgency.

I arrived at the hospital and found patients in various conditions coming and going. I called Tom's cell but it was unavailable. "Not good," I said out loud to myself.

"Sir, uh sir? The young voice of a volunteer was trying to get my attention. "Sir, can I help you?"

"I'm looking for the Maj…I mean John…"

"Are you family?" the young voice queried.

"No, um, I mean, yes, yes I am," I lied unconvincingly.

"You'll find the Major in the ICU sir. It's on the tenth floor—" the volunteer said. "They may not let you in," she called after me. I flew to the elevator thinking whoever "they" were had better be big if they were gonna stop me from seeing the Major. As the elevator opened I met up with Colin in the hallway,

"Hey man, you came!" he said surprised to see me.

"What'da expect? I fired back, feeling a mix of guilt and insult but mostly guilt. How is he?" His eyes answered my question. "Where is he?" I whispered.

"Room 1012, man." And then adding as I turned away, "Hey, set yourself. He isn't, well he isn't what you might expect…"

I didn't reply or turn back. Being kept out or scared out of his room was not going to happen today. I sped past the nurse station, predictably overworked and understaffed and used to family coming and going in the ICU at all hours. I found the room without incident and was spotted by Tom, his sister, and her husband who were standing outside of the room. "You came!" greeted Tom.

"Yeah, well I came. How is he?" I asked looking past Tom and into the room where I saw the Major's wife and three elderly men in suits standing around the bed. Tom…?"

"He's going fast," Tom said as he took my arm and led me into the room. The men, elders from his church surrounded the bed solemnly, one held he Major's hand, one had an arm around the Major's wife presumably to keep her from falling, and the other stood at the foot of the bed with eyes closed praying softly.

Tom marched me in and right to the Major's side. My mind raced as I stood close to the bed, the heart monitor, oxygen, and IV all in my line of sight, and then I looked down at the man I was told was the Major. A weakened shell of the man I remembered. My legs started to quiver. I struggled to process what was before me. What was actually happening? It all seemed so sorrel.

The Major half-opened an eye and seemed to recognize me. He opened his mouth to try and speak, but there were no words left in him. I touched his face and whispered, "Major."

His lips formed the word, "Son" then his muscles relaxed, and he was gone.

His wife wept softly held gingerly by their daughter. Tom motioned for the elders to leave, and I filed in behind the three to leave. "No," Tom said in a voice that reminded me of his dad, "You're family now. Please stay."

My legs buckled and I almost fell to the floor. No one had every said that to me. Not even my own blood-kin. "Tom, I…" He caught my eye, and I knew he was serious. His invitation came straight from his heart.

The funeral was prompt since it was already planned according to the Major's wishes. No surprise there. Even in death the Major was in charge! If Mr. Roberts attended I didn't see him, though there were folks from the retirement home, his church, and of course all his family was there. My head spun; I thought I was pleasant enough, but frankly I sorta spaced out for a few days. I couldn't tell you who I met or even what was said from the pulpit. If the Major had any influence on the pastor it was to the point, no sentiment just set'em right and get'em saved! That's the way the Major woulda done it!

I was scheduled to leave the following day. The rain that made my escape possible had quit and the job site was drying fast under a hot southern sun. When I told Tom my plans, he asked that I stopped over at his mom's apartment. It was the first time I heard it referred to anything other than the Major's. Life moves on. I really just wanted to get up and get going but I hesitantly agreed.

When I arrived next morning Tom was waiting at the door. "Let's take a walk," he said. We took a side exit and found our way around back to the fountain and could you believe it, there were two chairs, and the Major's thermos sitting on the table between them!

"Tom!"

"Just have a seat he motioned me down quietly. After Dad gave you his shotgun we had a very long conversation. Things on my mind, things he wanted to tell me but couldn't. It's was good for both of us, and I'm not sure we would've been able to do that if you hadn't been coming around. Really, this was the first time he loosened up since I married and moved away."

"You have no idea how much your dad meant to me Tom," I broke in.

"I know Tom said, but hold on, there's more."

More? More! I thought to myself. How is that possible? I'm not sure I can handle any more right now.

"Dad dictated a letter to you before he got really bad. He knew he would fade fast and wanted to, I guess get the last word in, you know?"

"Yeah, boy do I know!"

"Well, he couldn't write so it's my handwriting but Dad's words. He talked this all over with Mom, Sis, and me, and we're all okay with it. He wanted me to give this to you here by the fountain, with the thermos and he said, listen for the blue jays."

With that Tom reached into his coat and pulled out an envelope. I opened it and unfolded the paper, it read:

"*Well son, here you have it. I hope the squirrels and Blue jays are out for you. I'm sure the coffee is hot and Tom has done everything I've asked. Tough thing being a Father, you think your son is going to grow up to be a carbon-copy of you but that's never the case. All you can do is recognize that he's going to grow up and move on, try to stay close and pray for him everyday. Things had become a little tense with us when he married and gave up all the things I loved, shooting trap being number one. I had envisioned him taking over running the club when I stepped down but that was not to be. Meeting you and being able to talk out all those things helped me come to terms with that and, well life in general.*

The reason I came out there to the old club the day we met was that I was floundering around the apartment and stumbled onto my photo album. Slowly, I went through those pictures and started to release the memories and pain. Pretty much started with that hat, my First 50! I'm sure you remember the story. Well I started to let go of the friends that were gone, the person I was and would never again be and I had to make it right with Heath.

That photo album is a family heirloom and I want Tom's boys to have it. I want them to remember what their grand dad looked like, that he worked hard and was a man of honor. But there is something I want you to have. I saw the way you went out of your way to get Colin some work, and I know that had nothing to do with me or trying

222

*to get Heath and me together. I also know the last
few weeks before you left you put your relationship
with a certain attorney on hold for me and my
family. That was sacrifice and that son showed
real character.*

*That is what I was trying to tell you about
when I told you about hunting, building a club
with men of like passion and character, and that is
why I want you to have Curt's knife.*

I looked up from the note and saw that Tom had
been following my eyes down the page and knew what
I had just read. He pulled the knife from his back
pocket, took a long look at it, and handed it to me, both
of us knowing full well the story and significance of
the inheritance.

Now holding the knife, I returned to the letter:

*You see son, I can think of no greater reminder of
character than this knife. Keep it, handle it, and
when you are tempted to bend the rules or take
advantage of someone's misfortune, you look at this
knife and remember the man that came back for his
friend even though he was tired, wet, hungry, and
cold. That is something that can't be taught, that
has to be in a man's blood, and I've seen it in yours.
Good bless you, thank you, and God Speed!*

The letter was signed by the Major with obvious
strain. I couldn't speak for a long time. I just sat there
holding the knife in one hand and the letter in another.
Even sheathed it felt right, balanced not to heavy, not
to light. You could strap it on your belt and forget it was

there but in your hand it had the weight and balance of a fine tool. And I know tools. But there are a lot of fine tools in the world. This is a one-off, none like it anywhere and still that is not what makes its value. Its value is in its heritage, its pedigree, who had it, and why. I will never forget the auction and beating the Major's nemesis, Mr. Goode to rescue the knife from his clutches. Then too the days toward the end, and each time he spoke of the pain he felt over his lost friend Mr. Roberts how he would reach for this knife as if it gave him the courage to press on.

This knife was and is more than a sentimental souvenir from a cold life-threatening night and a very scared schoolboy. The knife symbolized through Curt Louver's unselfish actions all that was good in a man. It became the key to the Major's character in his pursuit of making amends with Mr. Roberts.

As I held the knife, I realized it was warm from being inside Tom's coat. Tom must have held it there a long time.

"Tom, I said looking up at his face for some sign of resistance, I really don't feel right about this. The shotgun was one thing, but this Tom, this is, well its part of your dad, who he was. Someone in your family might really want it."

"Yeah, he said thoughtfully, they might want it, but Dad wanted you to have it. You have no idea how much Dad enjoyed telling you stories and lecturing you about things important to him. We all had heard them so many times we'd just groan when he started one, but you were a fresh ear and that helped him a lot to come to grips with the things in his life giving him grief."

Turning away to watch a squirrel Tom said almost to himself, "I really envy him, he got to put all that stuff in order. We've had some good visits toward the last, so we did."

"Sorry, he said and turned back to me, guess now that he's gone I can think of all kinds of stuff I should've said to him."

Tom bit down hard on his lip and turned back to the trees. I don't think I'll never get used to seeing raw emotion in men. I really don't like it when women get all weepy, but when a man starts to lose it I want to slap him around, get in his face, and yell *Man up! Get a grip for Pete's sake!* But I didn't. I just looked at the knife and thought about a man of greater character and something the pastor said at the funeral about grace. Maybe I should look that up when I get home. Colin came around the side and called over to us "Hey you guys want to get something to drink? Tom looked at me and smiled.

"No thanks," I replied, "got my coffee right here."